*A portrait of Alexander MacKenzie, based on a studio photograph, coloured and framed for presentation to his mother in 1926.*

# FROM INVERNESS TO AFRICA

## THE AUTOBIOGRAPHY OF ALEXANDER MACKENZIE, A BUILDER, IN HIS OWN WORDS

EDITED BY

## JOHN M. MACKENZIE

Troubador Publishing Ltd
Unit E2 Airfield Business Park
Harrison Road, Market Harborough
Leicestershire LE16 7UL
Tel: 0116 279 2299
Email: books@troubador.co.uk
Web: www.troubador.co.uk


ISBN 978 1 8051 4288 1

British Library Cataloguing in Publication Data.
A catalogue record for this book is available from the British Library.

Typeset in 12pt Garamond by Troubador Publishing Ltd, Leicester, UK

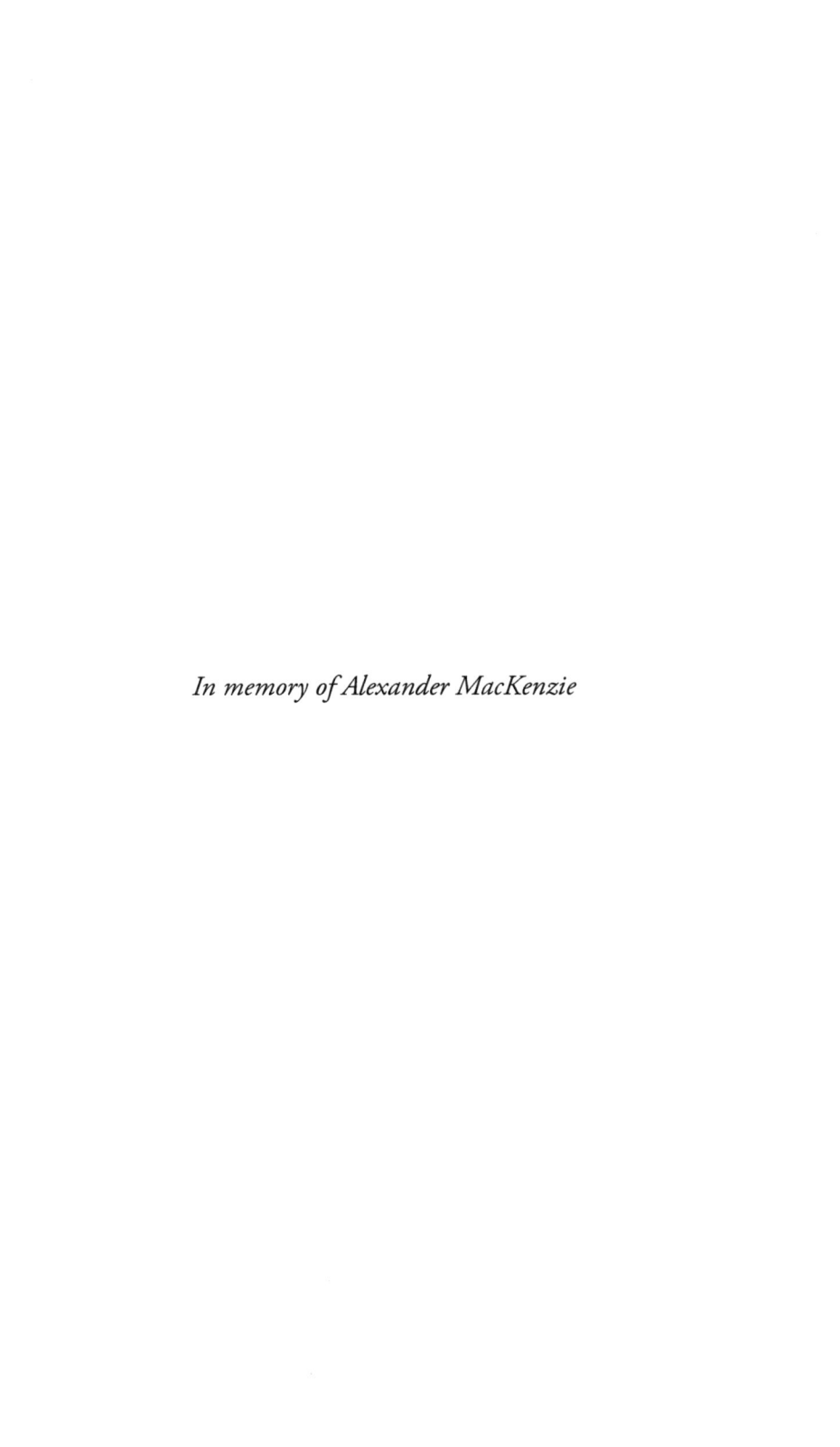

*In memory of Alexander MacKenzie*

# Contents

# List of Illustrations

These illustrations have been selected and captioned by the editor.

Cover illustration: Inverness before the demolition of the suspension bridge in 1961.

Frontispiece: a portrait of Alexander MacKenzie, based on a studio photograph, coloured and framed for presentation to his mother in 1926.

# Introduction

## John M. MacKenzie

In 1983-4 when my mother was terminally ill with cancer, my father nursed her to the end. His therapy at this difficult time was to sit at the dining room table writing his memoir in a school jotter. In fact, he seemed to have done this several times, another version being headed 'Memories'. Moreover, he also wrote a fair amount of material in a 'Quarto Triplicate Manifold Book' of the Northern Rhodesia Government which I found in his papers. Then there was more material in a foolscap jotter. All of this recorded a life which was remarkable enough to convey some fascinating insights into a key period of the British social and empire history in the twentieth century. In fact, although as related below he was very diffident and lacking in confidence about writing formal or official letters, he was always a very faithful family letter-writer and later in life he became almost a compulsive writer. He drew up lists of his employment with dates of the commencement and ending of the particular posts. When he moved to a sheltered flat after the death of my mother, he drew up lists of its defects, like the good clerk of works that he was. He seemed to have a passion for recording events and developments that he considered to be important.

Born in 1902, he died in 1987. In the years between, his career trajectory took him from straitened working-class origins through adventures in Africa in the 1920s, experience of the Great Depression and unemployment in the 1930s, activities in the army on the fringes of the Second World War, a return to Africa in the 1940s and then a striking progression taking him to the position of a senior clerk of works in the western province of Northern Rhodesia (Zambia). In the course of this period, he moved from being an apprentice stonemason, an apprentice bricklayer, a chargehand, then a foreman, a general foreman, an inspector of works, a senior clerk of works, and finally after his retirement from Africa, a consultant engineer's inspector. The latter took him to some of the most notable engineering projects of the day in Scotland, including the hydro-electric Cruachan power station and a major new graving dock on the Clyde. His remarkable progress represented ambition, exceptionally hard work, conscientiousness, loyalty, and above all reliability. It was infused with his desire to avoid the problems he had seen in his youth, including the tendency of some working-class people to drink to excess, to have no thought for the morrow, and often to gamble their money away. He always felt a certain amount of distress, sometimes of contempt, when he saw such problems producing misery, particularly when men made no provision for their potential widows or, in a very Victorian way, lost respectability by making no arrangements even for their own funerals. He was perhaps even more disturbed when he saw people whom he considered to have had superior social or educational starts in life throwing, as he viewed it, such advantages away. A quiet and unassuming man, he set great store by modesty and humility and rather despised those who did not demonstrate these qualities.

He was canny with money, but very generous to others, as I had good reason to know. He helped me in every way he could with my education and my travels, and I think and hope that I recompensed him by fulfilling his desire for steadiness, hard work, and success. In his later years he was most anxious to make adequate provision in every possible way for his widow and often talked to me about this. It was therefore sad that my mother predeceased him and he had three rather lonely years as a widower. During those years I visited him in Glasgow as often as I could and he also visited me in Lancashire, where he and my mother had been regular and enthusiastic visitors over the years. My brother took good care of him. He was overjoyed when I was promoted senior lecturer at Lancaster University and I was really sad that he did not live to see me become a professor, which he always said was his dearest wish.

At any rate, this account, largely written by himself, has been edited and occasionally fleshed out by me from his parallel accounts. In order to avoid repetition, I have conflated three or four versions written at different times. As already mentioned, one of these was written in a Northern Rhodesia Government 'Quarto Triplicate Manifold Book', intriguingly terminology no longer used. This contains various technical descriptions of jobs requiring to be done, financial calculations, and the version of his memories. It also seems to contain in my own childhood handwriting some questions that I appear to have put to him about his past and living conditions. In addition of this conflation of various (undated) versions, there are some additions originating from an interview I conducted with my father in the 1970s on my return from Rhodesia (Zimbabwe) where I had been interviewing elderly Africans on various historical topics I was working on at the time. On my return to Glasgow it occurred to me that the experiences of my father were also worthy of being recorded. Some at least of the revelations in that interview do not appear in his own version of his autobiography, so they have been used as additional information, as far as possible in his own words. All this activity seems to indicate a desire on the part of my father to explore and record his past, including the personal and national events that had influenced it. He was also clearly fascinated by the dynamic of change that had occurred during his lifetime. Since he had preserved a number of documents in his papers, it is apparent that he had the instinct of both a historian and an archivist. Towards the end of his life he kept a diary of things that amazed him, such as the great contrast between the living conditions of poor people in his day and what he regarded as being the comparative affluence that he saw around him in the 1980s. (He did not live to see the poverty and want of more modern times, together with the food banks where people could pick up free food. Had he experienced these conditions, he would certainly have wished to contribute to them). I have decided to include some of these diary entries because they chart his own encounters with illness and hospital and, above all, his personal traumatic experience of my mother's cancer and death. They constitute a sad commentary of the nature of old age and the realisation of the imminence of death.

In 1998, Nigel Dalziel and I published *Inverness & District* in the 'Scotland in Old Photographs' series (Sutton Publishing). Partly researched in the Inverness Library, it was dedicated to the memory of my father as 'a devoted Invernessian'. Many of the photographs in it were designed to show the Inverness which my father would have known at the beginning of the twentieth century. More information about my father (and my mother) and my interactions with them can be found in *Orientations: A Life at the End of Empire*, an Autobiography by myself (Leicester, Troubador Publishing 2023).

Memory is of course a slippery phenomenon, but memories are themselves important as reflecting the ideas and concerns of the person who sustains them. Memories from the deep past are constantly repeated, in the mind as much as in speech, and survive strongly, while, as is well-known, more recent memories can be more ephemeral. But all memories have some purchase on the person who harbours them. We can however be quite clear that the searing problems of securing and retaining jobs, particularly in the Depression period, imprinted themselves on those who had to endure them. Thus, as can be seen in chapter one, before he started on his excellent upward progress, he had to endure any number of short-term jobs to keep in employment. There must have been many men who led this kind of existence, and my father was fortunate, or very astute, to be able to escape from it. However, his progress was interrupted in various ways, by the inter-war Depression, by the Second World War, and by the retirement arrangements he encountered in colonial service. However, he seemed to surmount all of these and was determined to provide a comfortable existence for his wife as well as educational opportunities for his sons. It was always apparent that he saw the generations as having to advance, socially and economically each beyond its predecessor. He attempted to ensure that such was an ideal that he promoted and hoped for.

# Chapter 1

## Inverness

Inverness, capital of the Highlands, was a small town and in the years before the First World War we lived right at the centre near the castle. My first recollection was of being part of a small community consisting of about a dozen children in an area between the local police station and the town castle. This was when we lived in Castle Court off Castle Wynd. It was a three-bedroom house near the top with a lane down the side. These properties belonged to the minister. They were situated up a very steep hill leading to the castle taking a right turn through an archway by-passing the side entrance to the police station. The Wynd was a pedestrian public thoroughfare, but few used it because it was necessary to traverse five or six flights of roughly hewn stone steps without handrails in order to reach the river, which was famous for its good trout and salmon fishing. But sadly we had to move when I was about eleven or twelve years old. The city fathers had decided that the police station had to be extended and the houses on Castle Court had to be demolished. We had to move to a tenement on Bridge Street, not far away and still close to the centre of the town, about a hundred yards away from our old abode, but needless to say it wasn't comparable, sadly much less appealing accommodation. It was a very busy, steep and narrow street leading to the old suspension bridge (now demolished and replaced with a concrete structure spanning the River Ness). We were so sorry to have to move because it was a happy community somewhat removed from the bustle of the town. Our tenement flat was a 'but and ben', in other words with a kitchen and one bedroom on the third floor of a four-storey tenement. This was no. 3 of 11 Bridge Street entered by a narrow close about four feet six inches wide leading to a rectangular paved area, about 100 feet by 40 feet from which the stone stairs led up to the flats. This area was a great boon to the children as they used it to play their various games, particularly football for the boys. This was played with a tennis or other small ball as none of us could afford to buy a proper football, so different from children today whom I see all running around on fancy cycles. There was only one water source, a sink or wash hand basin for the use of all the tenants on the stair. Whether it was fortunate or not, this happened to be situated outside our door, convenient for us, but it meant that all the people of the stair, from the attic area and from the floors below, had to come to the sink near us. The toilet arrangements were even worse. There was only one toilet situated on the half-landing of the first flight of stairs. It was a very dark little space with only one small window looking into an adjacent close with no other source of light. We had to go down two flights of stairs to use the toilet. Such were the living conditions of working-class people in Inverness in the period. My Mam must have been very disappointed to move from our better accommodation, but she never complained. There was also a tailor's shop in the building. [Editor's note: my father took me to see this tenement in 1957 when it was scheduled for demolition. Empty by then, it was possible to go up the stairs. I can testify to the gloomy and spartan nature of this building in the centre of Inverness.] This close and old buildings are now demolished and replaced by a shopping centre.

About fourteen families lived off this close area. They were all respectable and hard-working, although taking a drink on a Saturday to such an effect that they were often broke for the remainder of the week. There was even an Italian who lived up our close and ran an adjacent shop. He was often asked for an ounce of tobacco on credit until the following Saturday and to my knowledge this was never refused. Indeed, it was an area where as children we did see the sad things of life, particularly on a Saturday afternoon when invariably most of the cells in the police station were filled not with criminals, but with mainly working men who had imbibed not wisely but too well. This was unfortunately a common occurrence in our town both in the days before and during the First World War. As most of the industrial workers finished working at 1.0 p.m. on Saturdays, pay day, the first port of call of the largest per cent of them was the local public house. In fact, I heard of one employer, a small builder, who used to pay his four of five employees in the sitting room of one of these hostelries. One of these public houses was situated directly opposite the close of the tenement to which we were compelled to move, so we could not avoid the drunkenness that seemed to be endemic then. I suppose some regarded it as essential to help them forget the hardness of their lives, but some of us found other consolations. The steep and fairly busy street led down to the old stone suspension bridge, now demolished. The police at that time were regarded as the enemies of the poor, partly because when they ran in someone who was drunk and perhaps liable to be disorderly, they were none too tender in the manner in which they controlled them or threw them into the cells. They were often regarded as violent, but whether this caused their victims to avoid coming into contact with them again seemed to be another matter.

There were six children in my family. In addition to myself, the youngest, there were two older brothers and three sisters. The two brothers, Donald and Kenneth, were already servicemen, one in the first battalion of the Royal Scots, which I believe he joined about 1903-4, the other a stoker in the navy which he joined about 1908-9. Their service was an indication of the lack of employment opportunities in Inverness, although the pay of servicemen in that period was so little that neither contributed to the family finances. My brother in the navy had a speech impediment, which was a considerable problem for him. The oldest brother, Kenneth, did most of his pre-war service in India and wrote home regularly to his parents. The sea-going brother however rarely wrote home, although we did know that he was a stoker on HMS *Birmingham* [Editor: a light cruiser] which sank the German U-15 submarine a few days after the war began in 1914. [Editor: U15 was sunk with the loss of all hands off Fair Isle to the North of Scotland.] Some considerable time later we received word that he had been wounded. I am not sure, but I think it was in some action off the Falkland

Islands. [Editor: since HMS *Birmingham* does not seem to have been present at the Battle of the Falkland Islands, this is either incorrect or the brother must have changed ship; in fact it is more likely that the brother was injured at the Battle of Jutland, at which *Birmingham* was certainly present, and there is a family tradition to that effect.] He got in with a bad crowd, often cabbies who were notorious, and drank a lot.

This naval brother, Donald, completed his twelve years in 1920 and took his discharge (or deserted) in South America, working for a couple of years either in Buenos Aires or Montevideo. He again got fed up and signed on as stoker or fourth engineer on a small merchant ship to work his passage home. Without any warning, as usual, he just walked into the house announcing that he was back. I found him employment with my old building firm, Campbell the Builders, and although he worked hard and his employer was satisfied with him, he got tired of working in the building line and within a few months he decided to emigrate to Australia in 1922. His mother received a postcard from him announcing that he had landed safely in Perth, Western Australia, but that was the last we ever heard from him.

As my three sisters were married and away from home, the main burden of earning was on my Mam's shoulders, so I had to buckle to and assist as my Dad was well on in his sixties, a stone mason to trade and unfortunately not in the best of health. He was frequently unemployed, particularly in the winter months owing to inclement weather etc., this meant that the heaviest burden fell on my mother who was considerably younger than my father, and she was one of the very best who showed kindness and compassion to anyone worse off than herself [she was the second wife, appearing in the census forms as 'housekeeper']. When she considered she could help, she would share any food she had with any neighbour worse off, and she would never turn a beggar away from the door without a cup of tea and a piece of bread and anything else that was available, so needless to say she was always a great favourite with them, also with the elderly ladies who came around the doors at that time selling odds and ends. I always felt that she would share her last piece of bread if necessary. My Dad died in 1923 having been born in 1849 and was buried in the famous Tomnahurich Cemetery, sometimes known as 'The Hill of the Fairies' of Inverness.

At this time there were two places of entertainment in our town, the Music Hall situated in the centre of town to which some of the managers brought excellent variety turns, and the Theatre Royal down near the river Ness where more plays were put on. Frequently after my game of football or some other time waster on a summer evening [although my father seems to have regarded football as time wasting, he was in fact talented, as we shall see later]. I would run down to the theatre when I knew there would be a fifteen-minute interval to all the shows to allow the patrons to partake of some refreshment, issuing a return ticket to those who wished to go outside. Frequently some young men who did not wish to see the end of the show (or considered it poor quality) would give their return tickets to boys waiting outside the entrance. In this way my pals and I used to gain access to the theatre otherwise closed to us and we would sometimes have a great laugh. These tickets would get us into the stalls, the circle or the gods. The show, however, often did not finish until 10.30 and this caused further trouble with my Dad who used on occasion to lock my bedroom door which was on the other side of the landing on the common stair, but sometime later when my mother thought he was asleep she would get up and hand me the key. Around 1912, a cinema called 'The Central' opened in the town, soon followed by another called 'La Scala', where we used to enjoy the Saturday morning matinee for one or two pence, the precise amount I cannot remember. I do remember, however, that it was sometimes a problem getting even that very small admission fee. I even used to cheat my mother's change to get the penny. Times were indeed hard. The films were invariably cowboys and Indians.

The other problem was that the dustbin men called around our area on a Saturday morning and I had very strict instructions from my Dad to be there and collect the ash pan when emptied. All the residents put out their bins on the edge of the pavement in this quite busy street. Occasionally I would get tired of waiting for the cart's arrival and move away from my duty for a matter of minutes and on my return find all the buckets gone. There would be real trouble for me and certainly no picture matinee. However, as with many other boys my greatest enjoyment came from playing football. When I played on bright summer evenings I often would not come home until after 10.15.

So at age 11 in 1914 I started on a paper round which meant that three mornings each week I had to be out of doors by 5.30 a.m. accompanying my mother whose first task of a very long day was to be one of several lady cleaners of our general post office signing on before 6.0 am and not returning home until nearly 9.0 a.m. when on her return she would probably have a cup of tea and then go to one of the several houses where she was employed as an occasional daily help, in the days before the installation of washing machines and where her usual task was a big day's wash when employed by a family who were some very hard taskmasters. She would rarely return home before 5.0 p.m. having earned the princely sum of 2/6 or 3/-. She also went cleaning at the railway offices with a middle-aged unmarried woman called Tini Ross, whose father was blind. Then of course it was a case of starting her own household duties, and unfortunately being so young I did not fully appreciate all she had to do.

Still I did add my little share with my paper round. I used to take two or three dozen papers which I bought for 3d [three pence] a dozen [the *Inverness Courier*, the local and popular paper, I believe the last in the entire country to have nothing but classified advertisements on its front page]. An apprentice printer used to pop out of the *Courier* office with an extra dozen which he had stolen. On a Saturday

*Inverness Station frontage, Alex's portal to a wider world.*

night I also sold the *Football Times*. The man in the *Courier* office had a preference for me and on a Wednesday would give me 4 or 5 dozen. Other boys would then chase me and I would subcontract to them for an extra penny. Before going around to the Hill district of the town where my customers lived, I went to the railway station where I used to catch the railway men going to work as they had a 6.0 a.m. start in those days, and also await the arrival of a naval train called 'the Jellicoe' which used to run between Scapa Flow where at that time a lot of the home fleet was based, and Portsmouth. [Editor: the Jellicoe Express ran between Thurso and London Euston, connecting to the main southern naval bases.] But I never sold many to these men. Then I would run up to the Hill district to deliver to my customers, this I can assure you was not too pleasant during the winter and black-out days. Some were waiting for the paper and would pay me on the spot. With others I used to have to go back to try to get the money. Unfortunately, some days I was greedy and would buy more papers at the *Courier* office than I was able to sell before 8.30 a.m. which was the ideal time to finish to enable me to run to the bakery to get a couple of rolls for breakfast and dash home have a cup of tea and a wash and get to school by 9.0 a.m., the school being a good ten minutes run from where I lived, so as I had to pay for papers before receiving them and they would not accept any returns I would endeavour to sell every one of them, which would keep me that little bit later. As our deputy headmaster was very strict on punctuality, at the last stroke of 9.0 the outer doors were closed and all latecomers were lined up and punished for sleeping in, which needless to say annoyed me having been out since 5.30 a.m. However, as I was late, I always accepted punishment which I am pleased to say was not a frequent occurrence. I was always aware of the fact that other boys at the school were better off than I was. I originally went to the Farraline Park school, but my father fell out with the headmaster and I went to the 'High'.

I often remember one particular incident which occurred one wet and very cold winter morning during the black-out. A lone young soldier got off the overnight train from the south and enquired directions to the Cameron barracks, he must have done his initial training at the depot probably some considerable time previously, but owing to the darkness of the morning was not sure in which direction it lay. As soon as I told him the way to the best of my ability he hurried on no doubt hungry and very tired as there was very little comfort on those trains from the south coming north overnight at

*A busy platform on Inverness Station.*

this time, even today there is room for great improvement, and while going around my paper round I wondered how the young man was getting on after finding the barracks and hoping that he had not overstayed his leave and that all was well with him. [This was typical of my father's thoughtfulness and concern about others. When looking at buildings and other constructions, he would often think of the men 'who built this'. 'All dead now', he would reflect.]

After my stint at school, I would hurry home to start my other job as a messenger to a provision and wine merchant in our town. This was in 1912 and the shop was Jacks the Grocer. The grocer lived at Ballifeary, had four sons, and had a terrible cough. His wife was English and was a great toff. He had a big house far above his station, which his wife insisted upon. He opened the shop at 8.0 and sometimes stayed open until late. As we did not finish school until 4.15 p.m. I had to rush home to start again at 4.30 after a cup of tea. We would rarely finish our messenger duties until 7.30 except at periods such as near Christmas or when spirits and wine stocks were low we would have to carry on until after 9.0 p.m. sometimes labelling and corking wines and spirits and of course Saturday was always an exception as on that day we rarely finished before 10.0 p.m. and I will always remember some very thoughtless customers who would ring up after 8.0 p.m. for some provisions they had forgotten to order and wanted delivered that evening, and as one of these thoughtless people lived over two miles from the shop and through a densely wooded area and with long drive up to the house you can understand the anxiety of the other messenger and myself on returning to the shop and told that one of us had to go with this errand on a very dark and stormy night and with a cycle supplied by our employer that was antiquated and with lights no better than candlepower, and all this endeavour for the weekly sum of 3/- or was it 2/6? We were always very much made aware of the class hierarchies in the town. For example, when delivering we had to be very careful to go to the correct door of the house, never the front or posh one, but to go round to the back to the 'tradesman's entrance'. Most of the middle class were always aware of their status and were very dismissive of anyone they regarded as inferior to themselves and therefore in a menial role. Perhaps unfortunately on the evenings I finished work at 7.30 p.m. instead of getting on with my school homework during the bright summer evenings I would go to the public park about one mile from my home and play football until after 10.0 p.m and then get into trouble with my Dad for being out so late.

*The High School, Inverness, Alex's primary school.*

All the schools in my town prior to the First World War allowed children to attend if they had no footwear, i.e. barefoot, except for the Royal Academy and the 'High' which I attended. It was called the High because it was built on a hill [Editor: my father used to relate this reason for the name 'High' with much merriment] and for no other reason as it only went to the third year higher grade and any pupils capable of and wishing to go further went to the Academy provided they passed what was then called the 'intermediate' examination. This footwear problem along with the fact that when we got promoted to a higher class and had to buy new books made things difficult for me and in fear of punishment frequently made me absent to the detriment of my learning when unable to buy the new books or footwear in repair, and unfortunately some teachers had that nasty habit of making a pupil in this category feel inferior, although fortunately I think I was the only one in our class with this little problem, and fortunately not many unkind teachers.

In addition to my paper round three mornings each week, I would have to collect my Dad's hand cart which he had stored in an old basement cellar in our close every Saturday morning around 5.30 a.m. and go to the gas works about a mile from our house for four hundredweight of coke which I can assure you wasn't an easy task as on occasion the material was scarce particularly during the war there was great rivalry for the fuel and with the larger boys and youths endeavouring to intimidate younger boys so that they would receive their allocation before it was sold out, but I must say I was always lucky to get my allocation. I used to queue up for the coke, which was the cinders pulled out after the coal had burned. I used to pay a very pleasant man in the office and then got tickets which I handed over to the man in the yard who had large scales. We took our own bags and filled them ourselves, but I can assure you it was no easy task pushing the hand cart up a cobbled street with a slight incline particularly in winter with frost or ice on the cobbles. To supplement this I used to go down to the railway sidings to search for any coal which might have fallen off the engines to collect in the hand cart or hurley to take home. This was however punishable and we had to be very careful not to be caught. We had two big planks to run the hurley up and down to the cellar, which was about six feet below ground level. All of this burnt quite well in our large Dover stove which had six rings. We had paraffin lamps for lighting, although gas arrived later and we had gas mantles. The meter man came round to read the gas meter and we paid him on the spot.

The fire station in town usually had a man on duty. If there was a call-out, there were bells on the station itself and also in each fireman's house. The men came running and the first man to arrive got two shillings, the second one-and-six and the third one shilling in order to persuade them to run as fast as possible. There were tokens on the fire cart or fire engine and they were grabbed as the men arrived. Ernie Sullivan, who married my sister was one of these men. [Editor: I knew Uncle Ernie at the end of his life. He used to sit in his garden with a catapult and a pile of stones to keep the birds off his strawberries.]

Another task was to accompany my father to a farm outside town where the farmer used to auction his drills of potatoes. When my father was successful in securing one or two of these for £1 a drill, we would harvest it, then build a clamp at the edge of the field to store the potatoes in straw and collect them when required. This was perfectly safe, as I never heard of any thefts since the poor seemed to be all very honest and concerned about each other at that time. Another way of getting produce was to grow potatoes and cabbage on plots at Bruce Gardens near the public park. We had two plots before and during the First World War. I used to help to dig a pit, in which we buried the vegetables. and covered it with straw and soil. I also helped with the planting and lifting. I used to use the hand cart to take the produce home where we put it in the cellar. Such items would last us the best part of the year.

Our diet consisted of pease brose. Pease was a very fine yellow meal which was mixed with boiling water. We had a meal store in Castle Street, where the proprietor was a miller. There was a range of grades of meal and Kingsmills was the area of the mills. I once went round to see the mill working. Wordie and Company was a great horse and cart man, who used to go from the railway station round the shops. We also ate a lot of fish, mainly herrings and garries [Editor: possibly 'garvies', sprats or young fish of other types]. We used to get a barrel of salt herrings from Kessock Ferry, but fish men used to come round with a push-cart with boxes on it. Wives of fishermen also sold fish and kippering took place out of town. An old fish salesman called Johnny Flukey (John Fraser) was always immaculately dressed, but sometimes there was nothing in his shop. So far as meat was concerned, the butcher often stayed open on a Saturday until 10.0 or 11.0 p.m. In the absence of any fridges, the butcher had off-cuts left which he wanted rid of and one of my jobs was to go round and see what I could get cheap. I used to buy a bone for soup. If poachers knew you, they would come round to sell rabbit or hare. Poor Johnny Fraser was on meths when he could not afford proper spirit. He went poaching and sometimes turned up with a pheasant or a partridge. Ferrets were used by the poachers. The police used to patrol the lane looking for poachers. Some got caught, but people thought it was no crime. Some took salmon, fishing in the river in the town. Although a licence from the town hall was quite cheap, some fished all night, particularly on a Friday night. They generally sold the salmon to the fishmonger. Often poachers made money just to go drinking.

*Friar's Shott and fishing on the River Ness.*

Despite this diet, some people virtually lived on pease brose. Johnny Macmillan whose mother was a widow virtually did so and they lived in the attic, with low ceilings keeping their heads bent. Johnny loved animals and when the circus was in town he would stay out until 2 or 3 in the morning. This big circus came once or twice a year and a big tent was put up in the park. I only went once. There was also a big funfair with many side shows, which was very popular. The sight of the circus coming through town with all the horses etc. was always very popular with spectators. There were also drovers (my uncle was one) who brought animals through the town to sell at the cattle sales. There were sales on Tuesdays and Fridays at Hamilton's and there was always a pub opposite. So far as animals were concerned, I remember there were two taxidermists in town. One was called Maclay on Church Street and there were always stuffed animals in the window.

The other major entertainment was of course football. All the men went, either to Inverness Caledonian, or Caleys, who played at the Citadel, and Inverness Thistle who played at Clachnacuddin. These teams played in the Highland League with other teams like Elgin City, Buckie, Forres etc.

During 1914 when war was declared and mobilisation of troops began my eldest brother's regiment the Royal Scots was recalled from their Indian station, at least the first battalion was, and also some battalions of the Cameron Highlanders and then soon drafted to France. In 1915 my brother got special leave to get married but unfortunately something occurred which prevented this taking place, and probably he did not wish to return to his unit again as a single man after getting special leave for this event. Nevertheless, he left home in good time for the return to his unit, but he told me that he got intoxicated in London losing most of his equipment, in those days all service men on leave from France had their rifle plus other equipment with them and whether he lost his rifle or not I do not know. However, he did not return to his unit on time, so on being court-martialled for desertion got quite a heavy sentence which he did not complete as after some months he was sent to either Salonica or Mesopotamia, I cannot remember which. We had a letter from his commanding officer saying that he was most surprised that he had overstayed his leave as he had done some excellent work with the company and younger soldiers and in fact he had considered recommending him for mention in despatches, prior to him going on leave. We often had redcaps [military police] coming round to the house looking for him. He did come back after the war and worked for Melvin the Baker. He was called up in the Second World War, but he died comparatively young in the 1940s.

For a period, I always went to Sunday school, sometimes twice a day, at the Castle Street mission. Major (retd.) Lockie ran the Sunday School at the mission, but the hall was knocked down flat by a landslide in 1912. Ness Bank Church was a higher-class place for the elite and working-class people did not go there. Nearby was another church, where there was old Machreghen, as he was called (did not know his real name) and he was a great old man. Working-class people went there. His son was killed in 1914. All this is demolished now. [Presumably my father was referring to the distinction between the established Church of Scotland and the Free Church, but he never referred to these differences.] There may have been missionaries, but their activities were always in the evening, and I never went because I was more interested in football.

My father, another Kenneth, was always interested in travel and in places far away. Between 1910 and 1914 people seemed to be always emigrating to Canada and the United States. There were boatloads leaving every week and occasionally a ship would even leave from Inverness. But others went to Glasgow or Greenock and we were always aware of the people's departures. I knew many who emigrated and most thought about it very positively, that the streets were running with gold and so on. The government encouraged this migration, but many found it difficult and success did not come their way. A lot came back. A few prosperous ones came back for a holiday, but the failed ones came back for good.

After leaving school at age thirteen my first job was as a full-time messenger at the grocer and wine merchant where I worked after school hours. This I only did for about six months and left when I got an offer of a job in a small shipyard about a mile and a half from my home as a steam hammer boy. This consisted of operating this hammer with a striking force of I would think of about two or three stones and attending to about twenty blacksmiths who used it when they had any heavy jobs such as anchors or any such items to repair after getting a welding heat on the material. When such jobs were being done I have seen the buttons on my overalls become quite hot and if that happened I lost my concentration and the hammer would kick off due to bad operating, then there would be a good ticking off from the blacksmith. The hours on this job were 6.0 a.m. start to 5.30 p.m. and as war was on three nights compulsory overtime until 9.30 p.m. and then that long walk home, no buses at that time. My pay was twelve shillings per week, but I was so exhausted I sometimes fell asleep on the job.

After about nine months in the shipyard and when I was told that there was no chance of me getting to learn any trade until I was sixteen I decided to leave. I noticed an advert in the local paper that there was a vacancy for an apprentice barman in a local hotel, Union Hotel in the High Street, and although only fifteen plus I applied for this vacancy and got it, so gave my notice to my previous employer and started in this hotel with bar attached with increased pay, but although I was considered quite a smart waiter and got on well with my employer I must admit I was never really happy in the business because of seeing the way in which men spent their wages and drank to excess, although the hours of duty were considerably less than in the shipyard.

*High Street Inverness, a familiar scene for Alex.*

I always remember one customer particularly who came into the lounge when on leave he was an exceedingly smart young officer in the Seaforth Highlanders. He would pay us a visit daily and at closing time would give me a half crown tip quite a lot in those days, still I must say I always felt so sorry for him, particularly when he imbibed too well, and thought of his poor Mam waiting for him to return and no doubt wondering in what condition he would return to his home on the Hill, but unfortunately during those days of the First World War in 1917 drunkenness was very prevalent as public houses would only open for about three hours before all spirits were sold out, so customers would try and consume as much as possible before this happened. Some months after this public houses were kept open later when stocks were available I think until about 9.0 p.m., so after that getting everyone out was at times not an easy matter, and walking along the main High Street which was a continuation of the street I lived in I would see several half drunks obviously arguing near the entrance of the close where I lived so I would turn up Castle Street and go for a long walk rather than get involved in any disturbances.

After being employed as a waiter for some months I noted that some customers were paying for their drinks with five-pound notes. This to me was a lot of money in 1918-19 and heard them talk of the good wages they paid even to the labourers at Invergordon dockyard which was about thirty five miles north of Inverness, so after discussing with my mother I decided to leave my waiting job and see if I could get fixed up there where most repairs to the home fleet were carried out. I left home on the early morning train and got a job alright after passing the naval doctor as age twenty one, though several years younger, but unfortunately was unable to get accommodation anywhere, but on the way to the railway station to return home I met my brother-in-law who was employed on a tanker based in Invergordon naval base who suggested that instead of returning home I should see the skipper of his boat who told me to sling a hammock and I could start on my new-found job which unfortunately was not in Invergordon, but at a naval mines depot in a small village called Alness fully two miles from Invergordon, and with a 7.0 a.m. start meant an early rise as no transport was available.

This depot was very well protected with six feet high wire fencing all around the perimeter and with London Metropolitan policemen guarding the gates and patrolling the site, needless to say with the storing and stacking of sea mines in long continuous sheds after dismantling of detonators etc., smoking was strictly prohibited within the gates where there was a number boxes where each man would place his smoking material and matches before going through the search area, and of course if any employee was found with any of these within the depot it was instant dismissal. Unfortunately, it turned out to be a very monotonous job and to make things worse frequently when I finished my day's work I would return to Invergordon to discover that the lighter was out at sea either coaling ship or some other task and would not return until ten or eleven at night. Eventually another young man to whom I told my problem suggested that lodgings were available in a small town called Dingwall, about perhaps fifteen miles from Alness and from where a workmen's train left every morning at 6.0 a.m. in very good time for our 7.0 a.m. start and returning each evening at 6.0 p.m. This was a great help and much more convenient than waiting the return of the lighter. However, I did not like Dingwall, thought it a terrible place and the lodgings were not at all nice. This job eventually ceased some months after the end of hostilities and I returned home.

Another brother-in-law who was employed in the local labour exchange then told me of a vacancy for apprentice shipwrights at Denny's shipyard in Dumbarton a town about fourteen miles west of Glasgow which was paying very good wages to apprentice shipwrights that they wished to employ and considered youths from the north would be suitable and as they were paying £2.10 shillings per week and as lodgings were available for £1.5 shillings it seemed very good to me so I again consulted with my Mam and we agreed it was certainly better than being idle so I applied for this vacancy and was accepted. This turned out to be quite a reasonable job as far as I was concerned as I was sent to assist an old shipwright who fell while erecting scaffolding and was given work that did not require climbing and erecting scaffolding. I soon discovered that working on scaffolding was not for me since I had no head for heights, but in any case, after several months there the firm went on short time, three working days each week which meant that I could barely pay my lodgings, so again I returned home.

On my return I noted that the old lady who had occupied the ground floor on our stair had left and another woman and her daughter had taken it over. Unfortunately, we very soon discovered that this was not to be for the best as far as the other tenants on the stair were concerned as they had several intoxicated male visitors. However, fortunately they kept to themselves and did not trouble the other occupants of the stairs.

During these years I had developed my passion for playing football and had become sufficiently proficient at the game to have reached one of the leading Inverness teams, Inverness Thistle, for which I played for some time and was even in the team which won one of the local cups [see the accompanying photograph of the team with its cup, my father being the player on the far left of the back row. It is unclear what H.F.C. on the football means – Highland Football Cup? There may also have been a charity cup. The year 1922 fits my father's career who would have been 20 at that time.] It became a significant part of my life in Inverness, even although I was anxious not to let it interfere with what I regarded as the more important aspects, namely work and getting on in one's trade.

*Inverness football team in 1922. Alex is in the rear row, far left.*

My Dad who was nearing his seventies at that time and unable to do much work, introduced me to a local builder with whom he used to be employed with a request that I get a start as an apprentice, although a bit old for this type of job they agreed to give me a trial. I must say I got on exceedingly well with this firm and who paid me much more than I expected. I must say I worked exceedingly hard rising to chargehand on small projects and I stayed with them for several years. But one day we were rained off early because of very stormy weather, and I had some time to pass before tea-time and as I had to pass the local library on my way home, I went in and noticed in the paper called *The Glasgow Herald* that the Crown Agents for the Colonies were looking for builders for Kenya Colony with foreman experience and not less than 25 years of age. So needless to say, since I was very nearly 25, I was very interested and wrote after the job. I must admit that it was a great effort as since leaving school at thirteen I did practically no letter writing at all, as composition while at school was not by any means my best subject, in fact I disliked it and apart from filling in my working timesheet all those years did none. At this time I had something of a traumatic experience. All my life until this date I had thought that my name was Alistair MacKenzie, MacKenzie of course being my father's name. However, I had to produce my birth certificate as part of my application and I discovered there that my name was actually Alexander MacDonald. This cruel system was a badge of illegitimacy since MacDonald was my mother's name. I had known nothing of this and of course thought that the discrepancy between my application and this birth certificate would mean that I would not get the job. However, to my great relief this did not happen and I realise now that it was a problem that must have been quite common at that time.

However, I eventually had a letter from London inviting me to get there for an interview. This was of course the longest journey I had ever taken and it can well be imagined how a young man from the Highlands of Scotland found London to be exceptionally intimidating. I remember one incident in which I went to a café to have a meal. While there a drunk or drunks came in and I was so shocked that I got up and left, abandoning my meal and feeling very hungry for the rest of the day. However, I must have satisfied the men on the Crown Agents' interview panel as they instructed me to go to Harley Street for a medical which must have been successful as I got the job. This Harley Street doctor who was to give me my medical examination had three or four degrees after this name and I now consider that his initial test came as soon as he answered the doorbell, as he was accompanied by a large Alsatian dog which bounded out barking and snarling. When naturally I stepped slightly backward, he commented that he saw that I was a little nervous which needless to say I had to agree. On reflection I have no doubt that this was to some extent part of his test seeing that if successful I would be going to a country where animals of all shapes and sizes abounded. It would not be long before I encountered them.

# Chapter 2

## Kenya

It was a lovely sunny day when I left home and I settled into my third-class carriage for my second trip to London prior to catching the boat train to Tilbury dock from where the ship was to sail. The only other passenger in the carriage I entered was a middle-aged well-dressed gentleman and as soon as he observed the labels on my suitcase, he immediately stated 'Oh I wouldn't go there' and then explained all the diseases I could get there, but needless to say I ignored these remarks and advice. Although I had been to London for my medical, I was once again intimidated by the vastness of the capital, but I was excited this time in the knowledge that I was going to a new job and would travel across the world to get there.

The sea voyage to Mombasa Kilindini harbour was a great thrill as needless to say that I had done no real travelling before, the ship calling at Marseilles, Genoa, Port Said and Port Suez and I thought it wonderful going through the Suez Canal and having the first view of the Arab people with their camels travelling along the banks. The desert seemed to come right up to the banks of the canal. The vessel, the *Llanstephan Castle* [Editor: a three-class passenger and cargo coal-fired steam vessel launched at Fairfield on the Clyde in 1914, which remained in service until 1952, having survived both world wars] had to wait for some time in the Great Bitter Lakes before proceeding into the southern end of the Canal. I was also intrigued by the coaling of the ship, which I think took place at Port Said, with all the coal carried in baskets on the heads of the 'coolies' or labourers, some of them even women. It made me realise that however hard my life was, it was nothing on theirs.

On arrival at Mombasa all government officials had to report to the transport officer there who gave you final instructions where you were to be posted in the colony as you did not know this before leaving the U.K. My instructions were to proceed to Nairobi for which I was very pleased as Mombasa being on the coast was far too hot for my liking. At that time the train journey passed through lands where African game abounded and it made an amazing spectacle from the windows of the train. Needless to say, I was intrigued and thrilled, very unlike my Highland home. On arrival of the boat train at Nairobi I saw two men dressed with pith helmets, Sam Brown belts and military-type khaki uniforms, shouting out does anyone know a Mr. MacKenzie and a Mr. Sydney Leonard. They turned out to be two prison officers. We eventually found Mr. Leonard whom I had never met on the ship and stored his luggage, one suitcase only on the vehicle, a good thing he had never to go on safari up-country as he was inadequately kitted out, and so we discovered that we were to be attached to the prisons department.

We were both taken to the Commissioner of Prisons office at Nairobi prison where he gave us instructions as to our various duties and informed us that we would be temporarily housed in a couple of tents some distance from the prison until such time as suitable accommodation could be found for us, this was possibly just a test. I walked back to town after this interview to post a letter and on my return late afternoon I saw a pride of lions roaming around some distance from where our tents were pitched, so had to make quite a large detour away from their area. I knew I was now encountering the real Africa. I well remember that there was a Welsh carpenter who had an absolute terror of lions [as well he might!]. After that, I spent three years living in a tent. There was a Norman Murray from Gairloch who got a house, but I was the youngest.

Next day Leonard who was quite a bit older than I was as he was in the forces during the war was told that he would be in charge of the joinery workshops and the training of long-term inmates in this trade while I was instructed to take over a project which was started by another instructor a Mr. Dewar who applied for and got a position in the Public Works Department. He put in a request for this change as he did not like the prison service. He really had better qualifications than the other instructors being a former student of Heriot Watt College, Edinburgh and the son of a building contractor. I am sure that if he continued in this department for any length of time he would eventually be in charge. The conditions of this job was that each employee had to complete a minimum tour of twenty four to thirty six months with return passage to the UK plus three days leave for every completed month of service overseas after arrival in the UK, this being doubled for every officer who decided to return for a further tour of service.

The project I took over from Dewar was the building of houses for African employees. On the second day on this job an African came out of an adjacent compound to the one where we were building and stood by my little office door. I am sure that someone must have put him up to it just to see how I would react. He was a very tall broad-set man but I noticed that the lower part of one of his legs was identical to that of an elephant hoof. I took little notice and carried on with my task in hand. I learned later that this disease was called 'elephantiasis' but as I had never seen anyone else with this complaint in my three years' service in the colony I don't think that it could have been very prevalent.

There was a Londoner there who had been an RAF officer in the First World War. He was a senior instructor and was called Mitchell, earning £550 a year. Mitchell took to drink, at night and then in the afternoon. He was to be found lying on the floor and Africans thought he had fainted. I always tried to cover for him and said that he had malaria. In the end he was sent home as a D.B.S. (distressed British subject). While in Nairobi, I always read the local paper, and the name Delamere turned up a lot. He seemed to be the biggest local man and was always mentioned in the press. [Editor: Lord Delamere (1870-1931) was the most notable white settler who owned 100,000 acres of land and was a highly controversial figure.]

After the completion of this project I was transferred up country to an area called Rumuruti in north Kavirondo where the Public Works Department (PWD) were building government offices, and in charge of this project was another

Scot called Tom Henderson who had been on the site for some months. Tom was a very pleasant young man perhaps around thirty years of age but was more of the office type than an outdoor worker, so progress on the construction side of the project was a little slow for the liking of the powers that be, hence my transfer to Rumuruti with a number of native convict labourers to try to assist. Unfortunately Tom liked a good drink and being what was termed a first-class official was soon a member of the local club. The members of this club travelled for miles to attend their weekend get together. They all consisted of ex-officers in the army and navy and were always referred to by their naval or military ranks they held when in the forces, i.e. commander, major or captain during the First World War, and after hostilities ceased applied for land resettlement in East Africa and got thousands of acres free, at least I assume it was free to clear the land of scrub etc., and prepare for cultivation after building their living accommodation which usually consisted of wattle and mud walls and thatched roofs. I think they were mainly bachelors and appeared to be very much better off than the average ex-soldier or sailor, of course I am sure that most of them would have emigrated there around 1919 or 20 after demobilisation whereas the year I refer to was 1928 by which time they had had plenty of opportunity to get established. Needless to say apart from the odd game of tennis which Tom invited me to at the club I did not mix much with them as my main recreation was a kick around at football with some of the African warders after four o'clock in the cool of the day. My footballing skills learned in Inverness turned out to be useful. The Africans simply loved football and it was a wonderful way of establishing good relationships with them, a great help when in the workplace. When I was a masonry instructor with the prison service, I received a salary of £300 per annum. I also received £50 housing allowance but did not get it if I was in a tent. I discovered that Africans seemed to enjoy stone masonry work much better than brick-laying.

I had one alarming experience while at Rumuruti. We used to stop for lunch around twelve noon when a couple of African warders accompanied by four or five prisoners transported the lunch of the site workers from the prison cookhouse to the job, at which time I would return to my tent for lunch where Cheroge, a cook boy I had brought with me from Nairobi would have everything prepared and set on a small table under the awning of my tent clear of the mid-day sun. After lunch I invariably rested on my camp bed in the tent until it was time to resume work again, but I had not been resting many moments when I heard scraping noises coming from a small section at the rear of my tent normally used as a bathroom and for storing any excess luggage, when I pulled back the tent flap a large grey mongrel dog attempted to attack me, but fortunately for me he was too weak and fell back on his haunches snarling savagely. Not possessing any weapons of any kind I ran as quickly as I could to my colleague's hut which was situated about fifty yards away from my tent, a combined house cum office African style with mud walls and thatched roof as I knew that Tom possessed a revolver and had a store nearby for tools etc., so we collected a long rope and the African house boys and returned to my tent. I think that it was Tommy who managed to lasso the dog and then we all pulled him to the edge of what was an old gravel pit about fifty yards away from my tent where Tom shot him and then we just pushed him over the side. I cannot remember whether any endeavour was made to cover him up although this should have been done just in case any other animal would attempt to feed on him and so catch this terrible disease called Rabies as at that time there was no known cure and so anyone bitten by a rabid dog would die in agony within a few days.

Two brothers had a store in a grass hut at Rumuruti. They had no competition and so they did well out of it, so well that they used to a take a holiday in South Africa for two or three months each year. They employed a man from South Africa to look after the shop when they were away. There was also an Indian shop near the village. It had been there for years and the family made a very good living from it. I used to go to get Bourneville chocolate from them.

After about twelve months at Rumuruti when my portion of the work was complete, I returned to Nairobi where I was stationed again for some weeks on general duties. I did not particularly like Nairobi as it was such a large prison and with so many different nationalities, all castes of Indian, African and European inmates. However, I wasn't stationed there long before being out again on safari to a native reserve called Kakamega in North Kavirondo. My task there was to build a brick prison to which the local district commissioner could sentence any wrongdoer to a maximum of two years. However, I'm afraid I didn't get off to a very good start as some days before leaving Nairobi I received an instruction from him that as he was collecting taxes at Chief Manubi's camp which he stated was on a direct route from Kisumu to Kakamega I had to call and see him there for instructions, but on leaving Nairobi my instructions were to call at the

PWD at Kisumu which was the end of the railway line and get transport there to take myself and luggage to Kakamega. Unfortunately, as I did not get this transport, a three-ton lorry, until late afternoon the driver was reluctant to call at Chief Manubi's camp as I assumed he did not fancy returning to Kisumu after dark as this area was all native reserve. I did not press him, plus I thought I may have to erect my own tent and other odds and ends I too wanted to push on (I was wrong). I realised later that I should have obeyed instructions and called at the chief's camp.

The district commissioner whom I met some days later turned out to be a very good man. He previously was a Colonel in the Artillery and reputed to be the youngest soldier holding that rank at that time in the British Army, but unfortunately got severely wounded during the war losing a leg, but when I met him this defect was barely noticeable and in fact although I did not see him I was told that he played a reasonable game of tennis. [Editor: presumably he had a prosthetic one.]

He lived in a large well-built four or five bedroomed house with servants' quarters at the bottom of the garden, and both being built of a good class brick the only other similar type of houses in the area were those occupied by the two medical doctors, a Doctor Thomson and a Mr. Harley Mason (I thought an excellent name for a doctor). They had their own hospital and were responsible for the well-being of all the natives in the reserve which covered a very large area.

Whereas I of course being just temporary in the area and a third-class official had my tent which pitched just about thirty or forty yards from the rain forest which extended for about two hundred yards, and beyond this the temporary prison was built to house the prisoners who were to be employed on the building of the new permanent jail. A road about ten feet wide had been cut through this dense forest area possibly some years before I got there, but if anyone had occasion to use this road, like the prisoners and the askari guards had to each day, even at high noon the trees were so high and dense that it was semi-dark.

On being transferred to Kakamega I asked my native cook whom I found reasonably good if he was willing to work there and he agreed, but we were not there very long before he suggested that he required a house boy to assist him with his duties as the only provision shop in the area, an Indian general store, was some considerable distance from our camp I agreed to this request, but the house boy was only a few weeks with me when he suggested that I should also employ a toto, that is a young boy, to go for any messages etc., this request needless to say I thought ridiculous as there we were with a primitive mud-built kitchen with a thatched roof plus my tent to clean out each day and another little mud-built hut with a thatched roof furnished with a small camp equipment table and two chairs where I occasionally had a meal. However, I eventually agreed to this request as I realised that if my cook left I would have great difficulty in getting another one in this outlandish area (he also knew this) and no doubt seeing the servants of the DC and the two doctors with white 'Kausa' overalls and hats this was their next request which needless to say I had to agree to all on a salary of £300 per annum, still being careful I managed nicely on this sum and also left £6 per month for my Mam.

*Alex in Kenya, 1920s, with servant boy known locally as a 'Toto'.*

I never knew where my servants lived as there was no accommodation for them nearby my camp, hence their great haste to dish up my dinner as soon as possible after 5.30 to enable them to get to their living quarters before darkness fell around 6.30 except on moonlit evenings. Very soon after darkness fell there was a great noise at all times, first with the croaking of I would imagine hundreds of bull frogs, then the roaring of Mr. Hyena, plus wild dog and jackal and with the occasional leopard giving a roar, but I must say that it was the bullfrogs who made the greatest din. At first I must admit that not possessing any weapon of any kind and of hearing any movement outside my tent I did feel a little nervous lying under my mosquito net which we had to use at all times because mosquitoes were very numerous around this area but I was very fortunate in not getting malaria as I was very often bitten but by good grace perhaps not by malaria carrying mosquitoes. But one thing that strikes me as being very stupid on my part, that was omitting to buy a chamber pot as very often in the middle of the night I would have to clamber out of my mosquito net and tent in pitch darkness to urinate and on several occasions could hear animals dash away as I opened the flap of my tent, what kind they were I had no idea as needless to say in the pitch darkness I could not see, but fortunately they seemed just as nervous as I was.

The site for the new prison which we were to build was some considerable distance away from my camp, fully half a mile away on low lying ground with a dense overgrowth of long lush grass and small trees which we very soon cleared but not before there was the occasional shout from some of the African labour 'eko noka' Swahili for a snake, and then there would be great excitement and noise until they either killed it or it managed to get away.

After the excavation of foundations and pouring of concrete, building began and of course our main task as instructors was to teach the long-term prisoners with a minimum sentence of five years to become capable on release of earning their livelihood honestly as a tradesman. Work went along reasonably well without any interference from the District Commissioner who was the boss of all government officials who came to his district. He was a proper officer and gentleman and on returning to my tent occasionally after my day's work there would be a note inviting me to dinner. I'm afraid I was not at all keen although naturally I appreciated very much the kindness of himself and also his wife, although I will always remember the first invitation to dinner at 7.0 p.m. When I arrived, I discovered that as was their custom they were suitably attired for the occasion while I arrived in my khaki drill. However, I could see that he did his utmost to make feel at ease no doubt realising that I was not accustomed to dressing for dinner and such a display of cutlery and finger bowls that I had never seen in my life before, so different from the room and kitchen house I lived in with my Mam. In hindsight I realise that I should have been honest and explained that I had not been accustomed to such a display of cutlery and before dinner olives and wines, however to me it was an ordeal although given a lovely meal and hospitable treatment I must admit I would have preferred my own working man's meal served up in my old straw-roofed hut. On leaving the D.C.'s house after dinner about 9.0 p.m. it was one of those pitch dark nights and as my tent was pitched just about two hundred yards away I thought I would have had no difficulty in finding it, however as I heard the movement of some animal coming closer to me than I wished I turned round once or twice and then lo and behold realised that I was unsure in which direction my tent was situated as my sense of direction was never good, and this was aggravated by the pitch blackness of the night. However, needless to say I was delighted when I eventually stumbled across it, on reflection later I think the animal which distracted me was a very large dog which belonged to one of our doctors out for an evening stroll but of course I am not sure about this as it was so dark.

But, to my embarrassment, the kind DC continued to send me invitations to dinner. These were very formal: 'the District Commissioner Mr. etc requests the pleasure of the company of Mr. Alexander MacKenzie to dinner on ...... with the opportunity to play bridge afterwards'. I used to get out my 'Complete Letter Writer for Gentlemen' [Editor: my father kept this all his life and it is still in my possession as is his 'Hints on the Preservation of Health in Eastern Africa'.] With its help I would send an equally formal reply: 'Mr.

Alexander MacKenzie thanks the District Commissioner for his kind invitation, but regrets to decline since he has another engagement'. At least that is what the 'Complete Letter Writer' instructed me to write, but I always found it hilariously funny since it was really impossible to have another engagement in Kakamega! [Editor: my father roared with laughter when he told me this story.] However, I did learn to play bridge at Kakamega and I soon felt as though I was as good as some of them. While at Rumuruti and Kakamega I used to see a lot of European hunting parties passing through with their rifles.

The only other alarming incident I experienced while at Kakamega occurred one Saturday lunchtime, a day on which I always had my lunch in my little mud-walled thatched hut dining area. While awaiting the houseboy to bring me my lunch I happened to glance up to the ceiling-less grass roof and there were two of the largest snakes I have ever seen sliding along between the thatch and the timber, simultaneously the houseboy came in with my first course of the meal and following my gaze immediately dropped it and ran away, needless to say I also rushed out closing the old timber door behind me, so as I did not possess any firearm of any kind I ran to the D.C.'s house to borrow one but on my return with the necessary gun there was no sign of the very unwelcome guests, but as there was a very large anthill just about twenty yards from the hut I have no doubt that would have been their abode.

The only other European who periodically lived in Kakamega native reserve, calling there about twice a year and staying for two or three weeks each visit, was a young South African recruiting officer either for the copper or gold mines I am not sure which, endeavouring to persuade as many young suitable Africans as he could to sign on for a tour of duty in the mines. He must have been well versed in the various native dialects spoken in this area to carry out a task like this. He was also a very pleasant young man, inviting me to his little house on two occasions for dinner. The other strange thing that happened there was that the Europeans were keen to find a fourth person to play bridge with them. Needless to say, this was not one of my sports, but they taught me how to play so desperate were they for someone to complete their table.

Another memorable event there was that the Europeans persuaded me to go out shooting with them, which was their favourite occupation. Every white person in the colony seemed to be mad about hunting and shooting since wild animals seemed to be so numerous. All had rifles and I remember one professional hunter. He lived in the Nairobi YMCA which always seemed to me to be a vast place with dozens of rooms. I sometimes stayed there myself when I had no other accommodation and I remember that the warden was a Goanese person. The clients of the professional hunter whom he took on safari were mainly after trophies and took their kills to a taxidermist in Nairobi. I only went shooting once and although I was proficient with a rifle, when I took a shot at a buck I fervently hoped that I had missed because I really was not interested in killing things, particularly when they looked so attractive in their own environments. Much more pleasantly, one of the things that surprised me about this period in Kenya was the way in which I picked up Swahili. I had been brought up a Gaelic speaker by my mother, Catherine MacDonald who was from the Isle of

Skye. However, I had to learn English in order to go to school. Indeed, when young, I was often confused as between Gaelic and English until I was able to sort out the two languages through education. If we spoke Gaelic in the playground we were often beaten in order to convert us to English. Perhaps, unknowingly, this gave me a feel for languages because I picked up Swahili in East Africa relatively easily and could communicate with Africans in that language. The incentive was that ability in the language (I had to sit a test) was rewarded with a slight increase in salary, £50 per annum. I was sent to the D.C. to take a test, but he failed me because my language was not grammatically correct. However, I continued with the language and knowledge of Swahili really helped me in my relations with Africans. They were always a very friendly and amusing people and I loved having laughs with them just as I enjoyed playing football with them, a sport which they loved. I always kept my Swahili grammar and dictionary and attempted to use the language in southern Africa, where it was less appropriate, but a few people knew it.

As in the evening, early morning 6.0 a.m. was quite cold with invariably a heavy mist until the sun got up higher about 7.0 a.m. when it turned lovely and warm, nevertheless 6.0 a.m. was always my reveille time with the exception of Sunday which was a non-working day when I usually had an extra hour as my cook and houseboy did not return to my camp until that hour.

As my three year term of contract was nearing completion and I was having word from home that my line of work was available there in the building trades, I decided to write to the department and inform them that I did not wish to return for a further term of duty, so eventually I received word that another instructor was coming to relieve me and on handing over to him I was to return to Nairobi for two weeks local leave prior to leaving for Mombasa on the Union Castle liner, I think it was the *Llandovery Castle* for my three months leave. [Editor: the first *Llandovery Castle*, sister of the *Llanstephan* was torpedoed in the First World War when serving as a hospital ship. A new replacement *Llandovery Castle* was launched in 1925.] Of course if I had agreed to return for a further tour of duty in the colony I would have got an additional three months' leave in the UK on full pay.

Some days after deciding that I did not want to return for a further tour of duty, I encountered one of the prisoners called Cheroge [Editor: not sure if this is a mistake since his cook was also called Cheroge, but it could have been a common name.] who had a reasonable amount of English and who was one of a squad sent out some distance from where we were building the prison to blast rock and break up suitable aggregate for concreting. One evening as I was standing outside my tent after 4.0 p.m watching the different squads pass with their warders, as their compound was situated at the other end of the rain forest so had to pass my tent, when one lot was halted and Chiroge came to me with two pieces of quartz and said 'Gold, Bwana'. I could see that there was a small quantity that glittered but really was not sure whether mica or gold but of course to be honest I was very ignorant of any type of metal. However, I thanked him and he and his squad carried on to the prison.

After giving this some thought I reported what Cheroge had told me to the D.C. who suggested that I should stake a claim. I'm afraid I missed my opportunity with this as I was due to return to Nairobi in a few days' time plus the fact that

I was not sure of the procedure and all it entailed as at that time the one thing I detested more than anything else was letter writing, so I went to the D.C.'s office a day or two later and gave him the quartz that Cheroge had given me knowing that he would get all the information he required from the boys where they thought this gold was located and so stake a claim and get things moving.

A few days later the lorry arrived to take myself and luggage to Kisumu station en route Nairobi, and I could see that on the day that the transport was due to call for me the D.C. was very anxious that I left for Kisumu as quickly as possible. I often thought that he had some experienced gold miner calling on him that day to advise.

On arrival at Nairobi I was given minor tasks such as checking water meters etc., both inside and out of the prison until it was time for me to catch my boat train to Mombasa. The journey to the coast was uneventful, although as usual there were always a large number of African animals beside the tracks which made it a most interesting journey. Yet this was always treated as commonplace in those days, I do not know if it is the same today. Each passenger had to look for the carriage he had to occupy on which a label was placed below the door with name and destination attached. My only other companion in this compartment turned out to be a young English lad who along with several friends whom he had met on the ship and were on a trip around Africa East to West as a present from his parents for doing well at University, he along with two young ladies whom he had met on board ship took the opportunity of this round trip to Nairobi while the ship was lying in Kilindini harbour Mombasa taking on stores and coal, a task which took several days including the preparations and taking on new passengers travelling to the U.K.

During the many hours that it took to travel from Nairobi to Mombasa we got very friendly although I realised that we were from totally different backgrounds although I must say they did not make this apparent treating me as an equal at all times. On the train's arrival at Mombasa as they had very little luggage they went on their way saying we shall see you on board ship, while I went about duties I had to do checking luggage etc. On eventually getting on board and finding the cabin which I was allocated I settled down having a good look around the ship to find my bearings.

As the ship moved out to sea the weather got really rough and as usual being a very bad sailor I was very soon feeling sorry for myself. I was not long lying on my bunk when a steward came to my cabin with a note inviting me to again meet my train friends on the first class deck at the swimming pool. Needless to say I had to refuse this very kind invitation realising that they came from very different backgrounds to me and I'm afraid made very lame excuses to other invitations so they very soon ceased inviting me much to my pleasure, although they seemed very disappointed on my reluctance to join them in their games on the first class deck as apparently most of the passengers in this category were older people. They were looking for someone younger like me to enjoy deck sports and other pastimes. However, when not being sick I once again enjoyed the voyage, particularly the transit of the Suez Canal and the visits to ports in the Mediterranean.

# Chapter 3
## Unemployment in the Depression

After a reasonably pleasant trip we eventually arrived at Tilbury dock, London where I made haste to collect my luggage and take a taxi to Euston Station. I had quite a reasonable journey to Inverness my home town, but to my dismay I discovered after some weeks that my information that there was plenty of work available was wrong or entirely out of date. In reality I could not buy a job there in 1930 in the middle of the depression. After some weeks I noticed an advert in one of the daily papers that there were vacancies for bricklayers in Bristol in the West of England so rather than be idle for a long period I decided to pay my own fare there since as I was not signing on the unemployment register I did not qualify for a rail warrant. I was very embarrassed on the train to be told by the ticket inspector that I had the wrong ticket and had to pay more for the route I was using. I did not have the excess, so I had to arrange to pay it later, which fortunately was possible. That kind of hazard with tickets seemed to be common then.

On arrival in Bristol late evening both very tired and hungry I began to look for lodgings as near as possible to where I found out the building firm Wilson Lovatt and Sons of London and Wolverhampton were building this large housing scheme for the corporation. I eventually saw in the window of a good-looking semi-detached villa that lodgings were available, the elderly owners of the house seemed a very nice couple so I was happy that I could at last rest by very weary legs. In the morning I went to the building site with my kit of tools which fortunately was not too far and had no difficulty in getting a start at one shilling and seven pence per hour. I was not long in discovering how this firm had to advertise for men in the North of Scotland when unemployment was so prevalent throughout the country, the reason being that they were exceedingly hard taskmasters hiring and firing daily with only two hours' notice of dismissal, this needless to say was to intimidate the other men on the site knowing that there were plenty of men waiting on the side lines to take up these jobs, men desperate for work from all parts of the country. In fact I worked on a small gable wall with three colleagues, an Englishman, a Welshman and myself. They were such hard taskmasters that very few Bristolian tradesmen would work for them and during inclement weather when unable to work outdoors would have to wait in a dirty cold hut until it cleared when the whistle would blow to resume work, this stoppage occurring two or three times on some days and with of course no wages for rained-off time so some days although being on site for eight hours perhaps cold and hungry and only work three, so earnings were just sufficient if lucky to pay for one's lodgings.

Surprisingly as I was really off the tools competitively for over three years I really thought that I would not last long under these conditions, however, probably the foremen and powers that be observed that I was endeavouring to do my best at all times, and I was surprised when this job came to an end that they told me they had a contract going on in Bury Lancashire and if I wished to go there I would get a start. Bring single and having nothing better in view I thought this was preferable to being idle as unemployment was still very prevalent in all trades. On arrival in Bury I got lodgings with a very nice old couple who had worked in the cotton mills in their younger days and told me great stories of their experience and working conditions in the mill and even in the early thirties while lying in bed I could still hear the knocker up chapping on the bedroom windows of mill workers living nearby at 6.0 a.m. telling them it was time to rise and shine and later hear the workers going to the mill a lot of them wearing clogs (very strong heavy footwear).

After completion of this contract there, where, while in progress, there was also quite a lot of hiring and firing, although not quite as prevalent as in Bristol, I was told that the firm had started a large housing project at a village called Wythenshawe about seven or eight miles out of Manchester and if I wished to find my own way there I would no doubt be able to find a job, so again as no better jobs were available and unemployment still prevalent I thought I had better go there and see how things were. This turned out to be a much larger project than the other ones I had been on, this one with twelve hundred houses controlled by four general foremen and four under managers, each team in charge of and controlling the organisation and running of their own section, and with a general manager sitting in his office controlling and supervising the whole project and with a plan of the site on his office wall and many different coloured flags for progress or otherwise of each section, this method being very successful in creating great rivalry between the general foremen and under managers. This site was even worse than Bristol for the hiring and firing method. Each day at 2.0 p.m. the foreman came around paying off very good men, but knowing that plenty of labour was still available to fill these vacant places and knowing that this would intimidate other workers on site, if that were possible, to work even harder. Even under managers and foremen were just as liable to be sacked if not considered one hundred per cent. The firm had cost clerks going around each section weekly measuring up completed work returning later and invariably telling the foreman that he is twenty or thirty pounds or some other figure in the red, in other words telling him that he and his squad have not made sufficient profit for the firm. This to me and everyone concerned seemed ridiculous as there was never a spare moment and everyone worked to their full potential at all times. Similar to their other projects in different cities, the daily routine was the same, two hours' notice of termination of employment, the firm knowing that these vacancies were so easy to fill. I again was able to retain my job to its completion when I was fortunate to get a start on a Methodist chapel being erected in the new housing area. While employed on this scheme and job I was able to get lodgings in the village of Northenden where I met and married my wife whose relatives were very dubious about her marrying a Scotsman. In later life she used to laugh at the manner in which her brothers-in-law used to tell her that Scotsmen went to bed with their boots on. After that we both returned to my home town where I was led to believe by my brother-in-law that lots of jobs were available as bricklayers. My new wife was very brave to move away from her home place to Inverness in the north of Scotland, a completely new place for her.

I had not much difficulty in getting employment on a small housing scheme about a mile from my Mam's home where we were temporarily based until we could get suitable accommodation. We eventually got what is termed in Scotland a 'sub-let apartment' of quite a large house in a very nice district of the town. This house was owned and lived in by an elderly gentleman and his wife who found that they did not use the basement of the property which was originally the servants' quarters consisting of a large stone-flagged floor kitchen plus a very large cooking range, bedrooms and toilet with a nice large back green. We were very fortunate to get such good accommodation as housing was still very difficult to get.

However, although we were satisfied it was unfortunately not for long as a few weeks after starting on my job I went to work on Monday morning as usual and was told by some of my workmates that I could not start as they had put in a request for a penny an hour increase in wages and being refused all the building artisans in the town had decided to go on strike, needless to say I had no alternative but to return and inform Hannah of this further problem, however, they informed me that they intended to hold a meeting in a room where we usually paid our union dues.

Two days later another meeting was held at the conclusion of which it was casually announced that a Glasgow firm Cowieson Co. Ltd were building a hotel in a town called

Fort William about forty miles from Inverness and would employ any building artisans who were prepared to leave home and work there in preference to being idle waiting the result of this dispute. I needless to say informed the secretary that I was willing to go there. No one else volunteered to do so, Hannah agreeing with my decision as this dispute could last some weeks.

I travelled there next day and after looking for and getting lodgings as near as possible to the site, reported to the foreman who turned out to be a very wiry old Londoner I should think well on in his sixties. I started on site the next morning and discovered that all the other bricklayers and carpenters on site came from Glasgow. They were all very good workmates although I kept mainly to myself and did not mix after working hours.

After two or three months the job came to an end and old Mr. Rodgers the general foreman told me when paying me off that he would endeavour to get me a permanent job with the firm as he intended to speak to the boss on my behalf when he returned to Glasgow. I thought no more about this discussion, but three or four days later I received a memo informing me that if I travelled to Lochgilphead, a village in Argyllshire I would get employment on a site there and would be able to work as many hours as I wished over the regulation forty four plus good subsistence allowance and guaranteed employment provided I was prepared to travel to jobs outwith the city of Glasgow. After discussing this with Hannah we decided that I should accept this offer with so much unemployment in the country. However, I realised that on taking these jobs away from home it would not have been very pleasant for Hannah who about that time was expecting her first child and was so far away from her own parents and friends to be again left on her own. However, she was brave enough to consider this the lesser evil to me being unemployed and told me not to miss this opportunity and of course I also realised that my mother whom I have already stated was one of the very best would always be a great help and comfort to her if required.

After three or four months in Argyllshire I was transferred to Glasgow to start the building of a temporary school in the Overnewton district of the city, not far from the Art Galleries in Kelvingrove district. I arrived back in Glasgow on a Saturday so looked around for accommodation in the area as near as possible to this project. I thought the best place to enquire would be at a small newsagents shop to enquire if the owner knew anyone in the area who was in the habit of taking boarders. I was correct as he told me that a family two closes beyond his shop did so but thought they had gone to the coast for the day's outing. However, after a long dreary wait they eventually returned and agreed to give me accommodation.

I was again just about two months on this job when the firm's manager came and told me that they would like me to go to Pwllheli in North Wales where they were starting a large project. I told him that I was very sorry but I could not go as I had arranged for my wife and son to give up our home in Inverness and they were due to arrive in Glasgow in a couple of days, so he told me to forget about the transfer and to carry on where I was working meantime.

Accommodation was very difficult to procure in Glasgow as elsewhere, however we very soon got a service flat in a good district (Hillhead), but needless to say we were still very anxious to get a house of our own with Hannah going to various factors' offices while I was at work, but without success. However, eventually my old landlady whom we had kept in touch with called on my wife one day and told her she was successful in getting a large house and would be vacating her two bedroom one directly opposite the Art Galleries and that she would recommend my wife to the factor of the property as a very suitable tenant and as we got this house at least for a time our housing problem was over.

*The Clachan, British Empire Exhibition, Glasgow, 1938.*

In 1938, I had a very lucky chance. A large exhibition was proposed in Glasgow in that year. This was to be an Empire Exhibition constructed in Bellahouston Park on the south side of the city. It was to include a 'Highland clachan', a village as it might have been in the Highland areas of the country to illustrate something of the history and architecture of this part of Scotland. My contractor employer decided to use me because of my stone masonry experience and my Highland origins. We duly designed and built this 'clachan' and it was ready for the opening of the exhibition. But then it was suggested that for the six-month duration of the Bellahouston event I should be employed as a sort-of handy man to check the buildings and remedy any defects. It was a really enjoyable time as the Exhibition was so magnificent and it was very good to see the visitors exploring it and enjoying themselves. I always used to say that it was the easiest and most enjoyable time of my working life. It was also a great privilege to be involved in such a historic occasion.

Thus, I was very fortunate to be employed by this building firm for several years although at times I had to travel away from home for short periods, but still I considered myself very fortunate until the Second World War began and some of the younger tradesmen were excused military duties as they were building bomb shelters for the civilian population and started to be employed by our firm, unfortunately the attitude of some of them appeared to be to do as little as possible and as soon as the first sign of rain appeared they were very keen to rush to the hut to play cards and when rebuked they would announce that they were war workers. However, in early 1943 we all got our calling up papers and although I was forty years of age I was the only one of the squad called up. I omitted to tell my firm that I had got the calling up papers as I was not really happy with my squad. However, as soon as they heard the news they sent wires etc. to the powers that be requesting my release as according to the firm I was a key worker, but omitted to claim exemption because they thought that according to my age I would not be called up. However, I duly received instructions to report to Fort George, the depot of the Seaforth Highlanders for duty.

# Chapter 4
## Service in the Second World War

Our special train arrived later afternoon when after a meal we were all paraded to go through the usual formalities of being kitted out etc., plus receiving a large sack which we had to fill with straw to serve as mattress, then our section was detailed to go up the old stone stairs of the fort and allocated our different barrack rooms well after midnight and I well remember fitting my buttons to my denims before wearily lying down on my bed to prepare for that 6.0 a.m. reveille. We had not long to wait for the start of another day and the numerous activities to be performed before lights out at 9.0 p.m.

On the whole the six-week training period soon passed (and I was glad that I could cope with the 'squarebashing' because I was fit and had been an active footballer) when we all hastened to the notice board in the corridor to see which regiment we had been posted to. I discovered that I along with three very young men had been posted to an artillery camp called Arborfield a few miles to the south of

Reading and not far out of London to train as 'operators fire control'. This was a Royal Artillery garrison station and my photograph during this period shows a Royal Artillery badge on my cap. On arrival at this camp we discovered all the work we had to learn was very secret on Radio Location working in transmission and receivers, but of course at first mainly in the classroom from 8.0 a.m. to 4.0 p.m. each day and with note books collected each day and stored in classroom which meant that a slow student had no opportunity to be swotting up of an evening if he so desired. In addition to this classroom work we had our physical training several times a week plus of course parade ground inspections and drill. In October 1943, I got a few days' compassionate leave because my second son had been born in Northenden and I travelled there to see Hannah and the baby.

*Wartime. Alex with Royal Artillery cap badge.*

However, as part of our physical training, our time came to go over the obstacle course which needless to say had some hazards but on the whole I didn't find it difficult until I came to the water jump and when I came to it I noticed two young roommates barely into their twenties were reluctant to attempt it. To give them encouragement I suggested they watched me go over it first, but unfortunately instead of landing on the sole of my right foot the toe of my heavy army boot stuck into the side of the bank I heard a severe crack but thought nothing of it until I tried to get up, but could not do so and with a terrible pain in my leg, so the PT instructor in charge of the exercise ordered two men to carry me back to the hut in great pain. I very foolishly didn't report sick but lay in my bed and when requiring to go to the urinal in the middle of the night did so with the utmost difficulty. Needless to say at reveille the next morning I was forced to report sick as I could not stand, and on reporting at the hospital was immediately put to bed. When the doctors came on their rounds the senior man gave me quite a talking to for being so stupid as not to report such an accident immediately as by the time they examined my foot it was so swollen that it made their task more difficult. Between hospital and remedial treatment I was about five months away from my unit, on discharge from hospital I was recalled to the former unit, this proving that I must have been considered satisfactory as if otherwise this was always an opportunity to get rid of any unsuitable man through posting to another unit or regiment.

I may add that all during my army service I unlike all the younger conscripts used to beat the 6.0 a.m. reveille every morning by about fifteen to twenty minutes slipping out of the unlit barrack room to the ablutions which were always lit up, and so have my shave and wash in peace and then return to the barrack room to make up and clear my bed space unhurriedly and so prepare for another day's duties.

About two years later on returning from a five-day routine training exercise on the Welsh mountains, as customary I went to the detail board situated in one of our passages of the block to see if there was any special instructions for our unit for the following day, where I noticed my name and number with orders to report to our commanding officer at a certain hour the following day, of course all my colleagues in the hut were very anxious to know what this was about, and needless to say were awaiting my return after the interview, and when I told them that I was to be temporarily discharged on 'B' release owing to a request from my employer, but would be liable to recall at any time. I am sure that I must have been one of the very first to be released after Japan had been beaten, all my colleagues envied me, and of course I was glad to get home again to my family, but really I must say that I did not find army life at all bad for as long as a man attended to all his duties and did as instructed it was quite a good life.

After a few days' leave I again started with my old firm who at that time were very busy, and after working in and around the city for several months and getting tired of these small jobs I applied for and got a position as a training instructor at a government training centre which had started up just outside the city to give young men who had been called to the forces the opportunity of learning a trade on release from military service by giving them a six months crash course in any trade in the building industry, the idea being that after which they would be employed on the building of much-needed houses.

After about nine months in this job we, the instructors, were all informed that we were training too many men such that the scheme was finishing and so we were all put on a week's notice, but it was during this week another instructor who came from Hamilton a town not far from

Glasgow informed me that he had made arrangements for an interview that afternoon in a local hotel with a representative of the Southern Rhodesian government who were looking for suitable building artisans to travel to and be employed there, so as things were not too busy at that time I agreed to accompany him and get further information.

# Chapter 5

## Return to Africa

On arrival at the hotel where the interviews were to take place, I noticed that there were at least another twelve applicants sitting in the corridor. It duly came my friend's turn for his interview and he obviously had been talking to the inspector about me, as when it was my turn to go into the office he knew quite a lot about me although I had not applied for this situation not having seen the advert in the press. He decided before I left the office that although passages were difficult to get after the war he would get me one in four or five weeks'

*Passport photograph, 1950s.*

time if I finally decided to emigrate, in fact he advised me to sell up my home and take my family with me although listening to previous men he had interviewed they had to do a minimum of six months in the colony before he could arrange a passage for a wife and family. However, I had to refuse this generous offer as my eldest son was due to start his secondary education, which I did not wish to upset as he was getting on reasonably well and of course I did not know what kind of education would be available in Rhodesia and decided if I did arrange to go that my sons required a mother more than I did a wife, as after all I had already been through I considered I could paddle my own canoe for a while just to see how things would go and if not satisfactory return home.

When I got a telegram informing me that a booking had been arranged on the *Capetown Castle* I had to decide whether to accept or otherwise within three days. After Hannah and I duly discussed the position we decided it was worth the risk but as a precaution if found unsuitable on arrival and after trying things out, to take sufficient capital for the return passage. So all my clothing and tools were packed up into trunks and I prepared once again to depart for Africa, Hannah and my sons seeming very sad to see me go. After the journey from Glasgow to London, I changed for Southampton to board the ship. This journey on the ship was boring and uneventful as after leaving Southampton the next stop was Cape Town, but as usual being a very bad sailor I was sea-sick before arriving there. [There would probably have been a stop in Las Palmas in the Canaries, which was the usual Union-Castle route.]

On arrival and going through immigration formalities we were asked where we had decided to go to, whether Bulawayo or Salisbury the capital. I decided on the latter although some distance beyond Bulawayo, but being larger and also the capital I considered there might be more opportunities there, but as our ship arrived in Cape Town about the 24th December there were no trains running upcountry until after the Christmas holidays, but fortunately for all passengers intending to go upcountry the Union Castle shipping line gave permission to any passengers who desired to do so to continue to stay on board ship for I think it was one pound per day. This was certainly a very good concession and I am sure that most if not all took advantage of it.

We eventually arrived in Salisbury after a very uncomfortable journey as far as I was concerned with four (or was it six?) in each second-class compartment on which I think we had to sleep at least two nights [probably three or four from Cape Town] and with a wash basin in each compartment for shaving etc. On arrival in Salisbury a gentleman was waiting at the station for all immigrants who had no other accommodation arranged and after collecting our luggage took us by bus to a government hostel situated two or three miles outside the city, of which he and his wife turned out to be in charge. I was extremely fortunate to be allocated a room which was occupied by a young sober man who was employed in the city, but as he had to be out at work all day in the city and didn't arrive back many times until very late at night I didn't see much of him and really had practically the room to myself. I may add that the food was exceedingly good and the dining room and bedrooms scrupulously clean as needless to say this was something to be very grateful for, plus a very fair meal ticket system such that if you did happen to miss a meal you did not pay for it.

After breakfast on my first day, I hurriedly walked into town which was some distance away to see if any jobs were available, but to my astonishment everywhere seemed dead, and on making enquiries I discovered that this was quite an important holiday period for all trades, so I returned to the hostel both hungry and very tired. I repeated this visit to town for the next three or four days, looking for various building sites and especially nearest to the hostel where I could apply for a job. This was important getting a job as near as possible to the hostel having no vehicle or transport available. During this waiting and very anxious period one young man at my dining table informed me that there was an advert in the *Rhodesia Herald* that morning for building foremen for the Northern Rhodesian government, which needless to say I immediately applied for.

However, as soon as the holiday period was over, I got a job that day with a firm building houses at 6/6 per hour, this was roughly about 90% more than I could earn in the UK. After about a month in this job I noticed an advert for a building foreman at 7/6 per hour so needless to say I applied and got the job on the construction of a large hotel in the centre of the city. I remember the morning I started another five bricklayers also did so, two Englishmen, a father and his son from Glasgow, and an Australian, needless to say I realised I have some competition here, nevertheless I retained the foreman's position.

I was only five or six weeks on this job when I received a letter from Northern Rhodesia that if I was successful in passing a medical examination by a local doctor, who incidentally was also named MacKenzie, the Public Works Department in Lusaka would forward a rail warrant for me to proceed to that colony as a temporary inspector of works. When I informed my employer that I intended to take this job he along with all my workmates considered I was very foolish in considering travel to this part of Africa which was a good three to four days journey from Salisbury. Needless to say, I ignored their opinions and booked my seat on the railway and had quite a pleasant journey to Bulawayo, but as the train was not due to leave there for another two hours for Lusaka awaiting a connection from South Africa I went for a walk around the town with its lovely wide streets, these I believe were constructed like this to allow the bullock wagons to turn around without difficulty. On my return I noticed that my compartment was now occupied by another man of about my own age, who had travelled from Johannesburg and was also travelling to Lusaka and to the Public Works Department, but as he was a motor engineer to trade he would be employed in a different area to me.

The next day we arrived at the Victoria Falls station where a lot of passengers left the train to enjoy all the lovely scenery around the Falls. We eventually arrived at our destination after midnight the following day and on arrival at the local hotel which had been booked for us, the manager on being awakened now after 1.0 a.m. apologised that as he did not expect us he had given our rooms to someone else, however he did have spare accommodation in two rooms which we could have as a temporary measure. Telling my friend to await his return he directed me along a long passage with a door at the extreme end opening into a very large room which I thought would have been a dining room at one time, but as soon as the door was opened the smell of drink was very strong and it contained five or six beds with only one being vacant and although I was not happy about the state of the room I was very glad that the vacant one was situated nearest to the door. Although I was terribly tired, I did not sleep well, although realising that I would have to be up soon after six a.m., have breakfast and report for duty by 8.0 at the public works department which I was told was some considerable distance from the hotel, but fortunately transport was available. My South African friend whom I met in the dining room informed me that he was also not happy with the set-up, however, he intended to report at headquarters and find out what his job was going to be like. At lunch time when I met him again he informed me that he had no desire to give this situation a trial as he had left a lovely home and family in Johannesburg and had no intention of tolerating the living and working conditions here, that is to lie on the ground to do repairs on some vehicles since according to him there were no pits, needless to say for my part I disagreed with him and suggested at least give it a few weeks trial, however, he was determined to return home as nothing came up to his expectations both the living or working conditions, and told me that he had discovered that a train was due to leave Lusaka for South Africa that evening and he intended going just on spec to see if there were any vacant seats and requested me that if he was fortunate enough to get one would I be kind enough to forward on his tools to him at his home address which he gave me. I duly did so, as I never saw him again although he did write to me to thank me for my help and informed me that the Northern Rhodesia government department were after him to refund his rail fare from Johannesburg to Lusaka. Whether he did this or not I do not know.

The hotel manager the following day arranged for me to get accommodation in a small two-room wooden hut situated in the yard of the hotel which was occupied by another employee of the Public Works Department, a quantity surveyor who turned out to be another Scot hailing from a small Lanarkshire town but had lived and worked in various parts of Africa for many years, he was an excellent neighbour being very pleasant and temperate. I found that although Lusaka was the capital of the colony, after 6.0 p.m. of an evening one could fire a shot if so inclined in the main street and be in no danger of hitting a human being as after that hour the streets simply emptied with the natives going home to their compounds situated some miles from the town and the Europeans and Indians simply stayed indoors. Of course in those days if a native had any reason to be out of doors after dark he would have to apply for a special pass from the commissioner's office.

However my surveyor friend and I very often walked to the train halt to see a passenger train pass through the town going on to the Copperbelt, this being our one and only recreation, but I still say that I was very content knowing that I was getting along considerably well with the work allocated to me, and did not mind conditions at this hotel, although only temporary until other accommodation became available as the food was very good and accommodation reasonable.

However, after six or seven weeks I was told that I could share a new three-bedroom corrugated iron detached house with another government employee who had been quartered at the hotel but whom I did not know, so I at once moved in, although about two miles out of town and about one mile from the PWD works. But unfortunately I was not many days in this new accommodation when my colleague would order various types of wines and spirits and suggested the buying of new carpets etc. I explained to him that I could not share in such luxuries and requested the housing officer to endeavour to allocate me other quarters as soon as possible.

Fortunately, just prior to this the PWD had taken over an old mud and wattle walled hut with a thatched roof which was air force property during the war and unoccupied for several years, but as accommodation was very scarce the senior inspector of works with the PWD at that time decided to partition a section of it off into a number of small cubicles each about nine by nine feet, leaving an area about twenty by twenty feet in which there was a small cooking stove and which he thought could be used as a dining sitting room, with only furniture supplied a table and one chair in the eight cubicles all very meagre, his idea being that this hut accommodation would be suitable as a temporary arrangement until things improved for single men.

Nevertheless with rental only £1 per month instead of the £8 per month for a house this suited me, although situated nearly two miles from the town and other habitations, and with grass surrounding the hut nearly two feet high I still took occupancy gladly. As there were no servants' quarters near this hut, I only employed a young boy to light my charcoal fire and get any messages I might require, as I did any little cooking or washing etc. myself, but as there was a restaurant at the airport which was only about half a mile from the hut I frequently had my dinner there of an evening. I was the only resident of the hut for nearly three months, but eventually they persuaded another man recently out from the UK employed as an official of the government printing department to accept this temporary accommodation until things improved and his family came out from England. Unfortunately, about a month after his arrival we had a terrific storm of thunder and lightning with the usual tropical torrential rainfall giving the impression of hitting our thatched roof. So he immediately requested more permanent accommodation as his wife and family were due to arrive in Lusaka in a couple of weeks' time. As he held quite an important position in his department they very soon found him a two bedroom brick built house, leaving me again the sole occupant of the old hut.

How the department invariably managed to satisfy an official who was displeased with this accommodation, if one or two men occupied a better house, was that they would unhesitatingly transfer them to another part of the colony where accommodation was available. This happened to me on four occasions during my twelve-year service to accommodate a more senior official. This needless to say did not worry me as after my first three years of service I was appointed as inspector

*Alex at the bungalow of friends, the Prestons, 1950s.*

of works African housing Copperbelt which necessitated me visiting all the towns in the area at least one day each week. These towns were Luanshya, Kitwe, Mufulira, Chingola and Ndola, so needless to say it did not worry me where my accommodation was situated particularly as my wife and family were still living in the UK mainly to assist my sons with their education which we considered to be superior to that which they would be able to get in Northern Rhodesia. So I moved from Lusaka to the Copperbelt, travelling up the railway line through Broken Hill. I lived in Chingola and got my driving licence there.

The main firms employed on these different projects were Costain and John Howard of London and some locals, but I must say that I was very happy to be part of these African housing projects travelling to a different town every other day from my home base and being supplied with a Land Rover and African driver to take me to the various sites which were invariably situated some distance from the townships. The government were strict on the African being in charge of the vehicle and to drive at all times. In addition to the African housing projects I had also to supervise some minor projects in addition to several houses being constructed for European staff in different townships. It was a very busy job which I enjoyed thoroughly, the only problems being not sufficient hours in the day to do it as efficiently as I would have liked as once it came to 5.30 p.m. my driver was very reluctant to work any later as he had about a mile to walk to his home in the compound from the garage and was always very anxious to reach there before darkness fell, as he said that that there were a lot of loafers and muggers around his area after that time who would not hesitate to attack and rob anyone they met.

After this time, I enjoyed a series of 'tours' of work in Northern Rhodesia, with home leave after each one. The first leave was in 1951 when it was a great joy to return to see my sons. The younger one had grown greatly since I had last seen him in 1947 and we found that we got on very well indeed, often going to Kelvingrove public park to enjoy the putting green together, even although it was apparent that he was not particularly sporting and that his main talents lay in his apparently considerable intelligence and ease of working at school, usually coming out top of the class. It was a great wrench to return to Africa, but I was happy to do so in the knowledge that I was earning enough to give those at home a reasonable lifestyle. I returned to Glasgow for another leave in 1954. By this time I had been promoted clerk of works on a higher salary. It was now decided that the older son could fend for himself and go into 'digs' at the home of some very reliable friends, the Harveys of Radnor Street, Thomas Harvey having inherited an undertaking business from his family. Hannah and the younger son John would return to Northern Rhodesia with me.

For John, aged eleven, this seemed to be enormously exciting. I had been to Longbridge near Birmingham with the older boy Alistair in order to purchase a car which I felt the family would need in Northern Rhodesia. This was a small Austin A40 which we drove back to Scotland, but which would eventually be taken to Southampton to be loaded on the *Athlone Castle*. Hannah, John and myself travelled together to London, again with trunks and suitcases of possessions, to be sent to the 'hold' and the 'baggage room', the different categories of sending one's possessions to Cape Town. We stayed over in London for two or three days, the first visit of Hannah and John. Hannah was keen to see one or two of the sights, including Buckingham Palace and we went around by bus and taxi. Eventually we caught the boat train for Southampton and boarded the *Athlone Castle*, our ship for the two-week voyage to Cape Town. After our departure I was sick as usual, but Hannah was remarkably resilient and never had any such problem, so that she could continue to look after John. He was briefly sick, but soon recovered and seemed to enjoy the voyage immensely, particularly after he had found one or two young friends. We landed at our only stop at Las Palmas and took a taxi tour of the town. Hannah had always wanted to travel and seemed to get tremendous pleasure out of these days, while in the case of John I little realised at that time just how far these experiences would change his life and influence his future career. They also seemed to enjoy their days in Cape Town while I was organising the unloading of our possessions and also the car. The city was quite quiet at that time and they were able to take trams to places they wanted to see. Eventually we set off from Cape Town for the north, which turned into being a very adventurous journey, not least because we were doing it during the rainy season when many of the rivers had flooded and it was very difficult being able to cross on the low-level bridges.

We were now heading for Ndola, the capital of the Northern Rhodesian Copperbelt, to which I had been transferred as clerk of works. At first, we occupied a government house in Serenje, a suburb of Ndola. John seemed to be fascinated by his surroundings. But it was good when we moved to a government house in Waddington Avenue, closer to the centre of town and John went to his school. He

*Alex and wife Hannah in front of their colonial bungalow, Waddington Avenue, Ndola, 1955.*

seemed to adapt well and appeared to enjoy all these new experiences, not least Ndola Government School, which seemed to suit him very well. We soon had every impression that he was not only enjoying himself but was thoroughly responding to the education at his school. He made friends too. Soon after our arrival we found a servant in Alfred who was a good reliable cook and supervisor of the home. This caused Hannah to cast around for a job that she could enjoy and would keep her busy. She found an excellent one in the Ndola creche where she was soon making friends with other members of the staff, including the lady who supervised it, Mrs Kath Cooper, a trained nurse. We visited other towns on the Copperbelt, notably Luanshya where we had friends, who at one stage put up John for a week. We discovered that

John was also visiting other schools in order to play chess which was something he enjoyed very much.

However, we were concerned about John's education. He was too nervous to go to South Africa or other boarding schools. Moreover, our sub-let at home was a problem because the tenants had left. So it was decided that Hannah and John would have to go home. In August of 1956, having been together in Ndola for eighteen months, we boarded a train for Cape

*Luanshya Road, out on a weekend drive, 1956.*

Town so that they could return home on the *Capetown Castle*. It was a very sad parting for me, particularly when I went to the dockside to see them off knowing that I was going to have a lonely train trip north to return to work. I also had to move out of our house in Ndola into more bachelor accommodation. However, I was home again for some leave in 1957. I now realised that I had no need to brave the rigours of the sea and sea sickness any more, but could fly, a journey which at that time took several days with overnight stops in hotels. It was also more expensive than the ship, but fortunately I had reached the rank in which the government was prepared to pay. These plane journeys could take place either via East Africa, the Sudan and Egypt, with one stop in Khartoum I remember, or via West Africa with a stopover in Nigeria. After this welcome leave I returned to Northern Rhodesia, surprised that I had been permitted to have an extra 'tour' beyond retirement age.

It has always been a government ruling that when an employee attained the age of 55 years he had to retire from government service. A colleague in the same department would be 55 two or three months after me and as we had both completed just ten years' service we were allowed a modified pension, but I had just completed another two year tour and I was due my overseas leave, but prior to leaving I received instructions that I could return to the colony for another twenty four months' service before retiring, so needless to say I informed my colleague about this and suggested he write to the department stating he was also prepared to do a further two years' service in the colony. To my mind this official was a much better educated man than I was being employed in an architect's office prior to joining this department. Nevertheless, he was informed that he had to retire on his 55th birthday and that a booking had already been made for him to return to the UK. It was a great delight to me to be able to stay on and improve my pension and I was flattered to be able to do so. On completing my final two years tour of service I eventually caught my ship, the *Pendennis Castle*, at Cape Town on the 1st January 1960 and had an uneventful journey home.

As I was unsure of my prospects of getting another situation at my age and of course being aggravated by the long period I was away from the city thereby losing touch with everyone I had known in the industry, and also aggravated by the fact that the firm which I had originally come south to work for so many years had gone out of business. Nevertheless, I was delighted to be home once again and to see how my sons were progressing with their education. As I anticipated, it was not easy to get suitable employment, as being so long away from using the tools of my trade, I realised that I would be unable to compete with other tradesmen younger than myself.

However, eventually I got a job with a Civil Engineering firm as an Inspector of Works, but which unfortunately again obliged me to leave home as the project was the Cruachan hydro-electric scheme harnessing all the water power necessary from Loch Awe in Argyllshire and travelling through the mountain to generate sufficient electricity to supply a large area. This was certainly very rough and tough work which I was unaccustomed to, with massive excavations of tunnels and the enormous underground turbine room that seemed as big as a cathedral. However, I persevered with it for a period and was glad to have good digs in Taynuilt nearby with very nice people. I went to Glasgow each weekend to see my family, although the long bus journeys were rather tiring. Needless to say, I was very pleased when the civil engineer in charge of the section on which I was employed informed me that he was being transferred to Glasgow to build a dry dock and would like me to assist him with this project as an inspector.

This was very good news indeed for me as the project was only about half a mile from where I lived and needless to say I was delighted to get home again. It was a very proud moment when I saw a large liner, built at John Brown's in Clydebank, being manoeuvred into the dock,

*Elderslie graving dock under construction, 1963.*

its first occupant. It was apparently the *Kungsholm,* of the Swedish America Line. Knowing that my son John would be delighted to see this, I rang home and suggested he come to the Elderslie dry dock by bus. He came at once since he was very interested in ships.

*Elderslie graving dock completed, 1965.*

After the completion of this project which went reasonably well I was transferred to new road and bridge works only about seven miles to the East of the central city bus station but in the opposite direction from where I lived. It was about seven miles from where I lived to the west of the city, and about seven miles from the bus station to the site, making a total travelling time of fourteen miles only, but unfortunately as there was a forty five minute interval between buses leaving to the village where this project was situated it meant a 6.30 a.m. start from home and not returning until 6.30 p.m., a twelve hour day with an outdoors job during the winter which soon made me decide enough was enough, aggravated by the fact that this civil engineering work was in lots of ways very different from what I was used to in the building line, still I think that I assisted the engineer in charge reasonably well. At least he was very sorry that I decided to leave as this project was far from complete, plus the fact that I considered rightly or wrongly that a younger man would be of greater assistance to the young engineer who was in charge of the project as both the contractors' representative and his general foreman were men who in my opinion had to be so closely supervised that I had no desire to carry on, although I realised that by resigning from this job I would be unable to qualify for unemployment benefit for six weeks, the usual punishment for any employee leaving a job. However, I considered it worth the risk provided the firm would be able to select a good energetic inspector who would be capable of supervising the contracting firm more closely than in my opinion I was capable of doing. However, unfortunately I never found out how my costly (to me) idea turned out, whether to the young engineer's benefit or not.

# Chapter 6
## Retirement and Conclusion

A few months after leaving this job I qualified for my old age pension, so did not look for any further employment. At this time I also had my Crown Agents' pension.

One incident I omitted to describe in my travels was that when employed on these African housing projects and travelling around the different sites away from base which was always a full day's work in each township the government refunded the cost of lunch, so I always dined at the local hotels. At Chingola one day I was seated by myself at a table for four when two men obviously miners or surveyors with their loudly striped shirts, shorts and bush hats sat at my table so as we got into conversation they stated they were not particularly impressed with Northern Rhodesia, as they much preferred East Africa. When they mentioned this, I asked them if they had ever been to Kakamega district North Kavirondo. 'Oh yes' they said 'and that's the area we intend to return to as we don't like it here' and mentioned that they had worked on the gold mine there and although in the native reserve a township was built with hotels, shops and bars etc., but unfortunately they said that the gold had run out about 1938, but while it lasted there was great affluence and their boss finally left for South Africa with £80,000, a lot of money in the 1930s, still I must say that I was not a bit envious after their story that I had missed out on this bonanza, as this was the area where the Africans showed me the quartz. I must say that I never regretted leaving the colony and my return home, although I had liked the country very much, particularly the lovely sunshine and the solitude, just what I wanted and never going very far away from my tent during my non-working hours I simply loved this quietness and solitude. In fact apart from mixing with my workers during the day I was without doubt a proper recluse, but I must say that at that time in the inter-war years I liked it that way.

On my return home to the UK life turned out to be so different with the problems hunting for work and after being successful the anxiety of being able to retain it, and the experience of some of the boarding houses one had to put up with. However, I was so glad that I had decided not to return to Africa although I had to go through this trying and hard times of the thirties and travelling here and there for work since I would never have met Hannah my wife, for this I am very grateful as she has been a very good mother and partner at all times to me.

In conclusion I must say that in my humble opinion I disagree with the opinions held in the old days by the average working class parents that a boy should be held with his nose to the grind stones at all times as even I used to envy just a little some of the other pupils in my class making arrangements for and picking their team to play another juvenile team from some different school in the town on a Saturday morning and although being selected had always to refuse inclusion in the team owing to having to work all day Saturday in my after school messenger job, in any case my parents could never have been able or willing to buy me the football boots and strip required to be a member of the team, still I must say I was never envious of the boys in the team whose parents were able to buy them the necessary strips, but was so glad that I had a job and able in some little way to help towards the family budget at that time.

Still I am certain that it paid good dividends to those families who were in a position to let their children worry about home and school work only at that time. As I did hear some years later that quite a number of them held quite important positions in various professions after leaving university, although I never had the pleasure of meeting any of them, still there must always be some to do the unusual jobs and I must admit being in this category that at all times I have been satisfied with my lot as one of the very ordinary working men.

Wednesday 1st June 1983: In conclusion, what strikes me most of life to-day compared to my messenger duties pre-1914? While on holiday at my son's home at Heysham, a district near Morecambe, a Lancashire holiday resort, he took his Mam and me to a very large supermarket called Asda situated about halfway between Heysham and Lancaster in a very quiet area, yet the store was bustling with activity queuing up at the check-out, and although a very large parking area was provided he had difficulty in finding an empty space. On entering this store what really did surprise me was that at least seventy per cent of the customers I saw had trolleys which were overflowing with provisions. My son's was less than a quarter full, yet the cost £20 plus this trip needless to say brought me back to my boyhood days when I was employed as a provision merchant's errand boy and my Mam would await my return home with my pay on a Saturday evening, 3/6 I think it was in old money, with which I could buy sufficient meat and vegetables to make a large pan of soup plus sausages for Sunday's breakfast to feed my Mam, father and me for Sunday and Monday plus quite a large bag of sweets for three pence from a shop called Low and Leaf, a store which did not close before eleven p.m. on a Saturday evening in these pre-1914 days. It was called 'the Glasgow shop' by the townspeople in Inverness as this was the city where the main stores were situated, and it was surprising how busy they were late at night on a Saturday where the staff must have been very tired after a full day's work, fortunately so different to life today. Nowadays in the 1980s few would work after 5.30 or 6.0, although Indian shop owners work very long hours as do people in Chinese restaurants.

Wednesday 3rd August, 1983. I wish to record another little incident that occurred to me in my eightieth year. A sore appeared under my left eye just where my reading glasses rest (I do not require glasses apart from this), but I did think the sore was associated with the movement of my glasses, but after some months when there was no sign of improvement I decided to go to consult my G.P. who told me that this sore was not caused by my glasses, but was a 'rodent ulcer' which would require a small operation to remove and he would report to the local hospital. Some weeks later I had notice that they would confirm that I had to go into hospital possibly for just a couple of days. But unfortunately, after three days in hospital and after numerous tests of all kinds, the house doctor informed me that as the surgeon had taken ill my operation date would have to be delayed, so needless to say although conditions in the hospital were first class I decided to return home that evening rather than stay on in hospital. Four days later I received an urgent message to return that day and the following day duly had my operation, but what really surprised me was the quantity and quality of the food given to patients, very good in my opinion, but the changing of the bed linen every single day seemed unnecessary in my humble opinion for some patients like those in my condition, but I suppose that was the instructions from the powers that be.

Five days later I had the stitches removed although my eye and face were very badly discoloured. I thought that would have been the final part of the job, but unfortunately the pain did not go away. I was once again instructed to report to the senior doctor five says later, but again it was the young doctor who did the operation who just instructed me to return in two months' time for a further check to see if all was well. Indeed, another rodent ulcer appeared on my nose and I was told that these were a form of skin cancer caused by my time living in the tropics and getting too much sun on my face.

At this time my dear Hannah was reasonably well, but some weeks later she had to attend the doctor's surgery as she did not feel at all well. I accompanied her there when she received the usual prescription and this may have given her temporary relief, but unfortunately later on she was informed that she should go to hospital for an operation, this would help her greatly. It was a bowel cancer and she was massively weakened by such invasive surgery. When she came out of hospital she seemed like a shadow of her former self, but I nursed her and gave her some good food and there came a day when she seemed to turn a corner and became much stronger, almost returning to her former self. This remission was all too short and some time later there was a recurrence of her illness and at times she was in considerable pain and although her doctor suggested she should return to hospital she seemed to know that this would do little good and she refused to go, preferring to stay at home with me, for which I was very pleased. But this time my dear partner suffered for some weeks and her suffering was sad to behold, although she was of course given pain relief. She was ready and prepared to pass out of this world when the time came, although I had a lingering hope that she would turn the corner again, although my sons assured me gently that this was impossible. She had visits from her most attentive minister.

After this great loss I was completely dazed and did not really know what to do for the best for some considerable time after this. In fact, in my own estimation I was never very bright [here he means in mental ability], but at this period I seemed worse than ever. I always regarded Hannah as being more clever than myself and I felt as though her death had been like a brain death to me.

However, after two or three months my sons came up with the idea that I must leave this three-bedroom house with a very large garden with hedges occupying an end-terrace and which we had occupied for over twenty-three years, as they considered, probably rightly, that as I was approaching the age of 82, the problem of keeping the house plus the garden neat and tidy was more than I was physically capable of doing on my own. So they actually persuaded me to buy an old person's one bedroom flat in the same area in which Hannah and I had lived for so many years. Although we had lived in the city for so many years this was really the only area that I knew and an area which my late partner had really loved. She was very much brighter than me and knew most parts of the city, but as she had got to know a great number of the older residents in this area I am certain that she would never have dreamed of leaving it and the house that we had occupied for so many years if she had been left on her own.

I must say that I was not impressed with my new abode at first having no shed or anywhere to store odds and ends not required immediately, plus the fact that I found lots of minor defects in the construction which I had to get rectified by the firm's inspector who paid periodic visits to the site, in fact now nearly two months have passed and they are still not done, most are, but not all. Without a piece of garden or some other outdoor work to attend to some days are inclined to drag a little not being a book worm. However, tomorrow the 27th June Barret's site sales lady who has still six or seven houses to sell has organised a bus trip for some of the house owners, so I am hoping all will go well.

We had our day trip yesterday which turned out to be a lovely day with the intention of going to Callander, a small town some fifty or sixty miles from Glasgow, but unfortunately for the bus owner, the bus had a puncture in one of the front tyres not too distant from the Lake of Menteith where he managed to drive the vehicle slowly and we had a very good lunch in the hotel there, after which when he had the necessary repairs carried out we carried on to the little town of Callander where we spent a very enjoyable hour and after that our uneventful but pleasant journey home which I think everyone enjoyed.

[There is little in the diary after this. It will have been noticed that in all my father's descriptions he was very concerned with accurate distances, something characteristic of him. Once he had settled into his flat, his routine was to walk down to the newsagent on the main road every morning to collect his newspaper. He had always enjoyed snooker and he became an avid watcher of the tournaments on television. This was the heyday of Stephen Hendry whom he greatly admired. One day he nearly fainted on his morning walk and had to sit down on a wall. This indicated the development of his own cancer in 1987 and he died in hospital on the 23rd April, St. George's Day, of that year. His funeral was a very moving affair attended by several family friends, including those who had spotted the death announced in the *Glasgow Herald*.]

Printed in the USA
CPSIA information can be obtained
at www.ICGtesting.com
LVHW070755060624
782466LV00017B/245